D1556093

STOCKPORT LIBRARIES

C2000 00187 7079

# The Black Flash
## The Albert Johanneson Story

# The Black Flash
## The Albert Johanneson Story

Paul Harrison

## Vertical Editions
www.verticaleditions.com

Copyright © Paul Harrison 2012

The right of Paul Harrison to be identified as the author of this work
has been asserted in accordance with the Copyright, Designs and
Patents Act, 1988

All rights reserved. The reproduction and utilisation of this book in
any form or by any electrical, mechanical or other means, now known
or hereafter invented, including photocopying and recording, and in
any information storage and retrieval system, is forbidden without the
written permission of the publisher

First published in the United Kingdom in 2012 by Vertical Editions,
Unit 4a, Snaygill Industrial Estate, Skipton, North Yorkshire BD23 2QR

www.verticaleditions.com

ISBN 978-1-904091-56-1

A CIP catalogue record for this book is available from the British
Library

Cover design by HBA, York

Printed and bound by MPG, Bodmin

| STOCKPORT LIBRARIES | |
|---|---|
| C2001877079 | |
| Bertrams | 07/09/2012 |
| 796.334092 | JOH |
| CLL | £15.99 |

# Contents

# Acknowledgements

This book has been one of the most difficult tasks I have yet achieved, not simply because of the emotional aspect of researching and writing a book on a long since departed football hero and idol to thousands across the world, it has also proved physically difficult since the research has taken me around the world and back again.

Not only that, there has been much in the way of individual resistance in certain areas, a reticence to release acquired information and detail. So called historians requesting thousands of pounds for details about Albert, others have clearly felt threatened because the self referred 'expert status' they have bestowed upon themselves is pointless and meaningless. Having researched and penned several biographies, I confess that at times I have found it extremely difficult to understand the mentality of some of those who, by a reluctance to share, or who seek personal financial reward for information, are simply perpetuating the abuse Albert suffered throughout his life in England. There is no further need for me to comment here, you know who you are.

For far too many years, the achievement and life of black South African footballer, Albert Johanneson has been diminished to just two defining moments; he was the first black footballer to appear in an FA Cup Final at Wembley Stadium, and much later, he died a lonely, penniless alcoholic.

The reality is that Albert was much more than either of

those memories; he was a man, a human being who deserves far greater recognition than he has thus far received, notwithstanding the adulation and unconditional love his own family possess for him. Few commentators relate to, or consider, the reality of Albert's life and career in football, the vast majority of this work is in Albert's own words, it is his recollections, memories, anecdotes, his emotions and feelings, his statements that are being relayed within this very unique volume. As his biographer I am biased, however, on every occasion I met and interviewed him, Albert remained a gentleman, he was always respectful to his peers and I never once found him to be disingenuous, not even towards those who deserved far more scathing criticism than he delivered towards them. Somehow, and I don't know how he managed it, whenever he had been physically or verbally hurt or abused, Albert always found within himself to forgive and to turn the other cheek. It takes a special person indeed to be able to do that, I am not alone in knowing that Albert Johanneson was a very special person indeed. The hurt and abuse was one of the few constants in his all too brief life, he didn't deserve it, nobody deserves to be treated in such an inhumane manner by their fellows. But more of that later.

This work could never have been completed without the input and support of many others, not least, the 'Black Flash' himself – Albert Johanneson. I would also like to convey my sincere appreciation to Albert's brother, the late Trevor Johanneson, and Albert's two daughters who were the true loves of his life – Alicia and Yvonne, for the discussions and interaction from afar, and to their respective families, including the elusive (to me) Hepburn Harrison Graham, who despite my best efforts, I never quite got to meet. To Mandy, Paula, Mark, Mia, Thomas, Amber, Angel, George and the Harrison family's very own Black Flash – the late great Bingo. Great appreciation must go to: Luke Martyn Alfred, Sports Editor of the *Johannesburg Times* who was an incredible inspiration and an all round supportive person, the late Keith Alexander, Ruth Johnson and Howard Holmes at Football United – Racism Divides, Danny Lynch at Kick it Out, Chrischene at District Six Museum (South Africa), the Football League, Guy, Julian Rod – site editor at www.expro.co.za, Kenny Eagles who is from one of South Africa's most eminent football families, Thom Kirwin at Yorkshire Radio. Sincere appreciation goes to the following, many of whom are sadly no longer with us; Don Revie, Billy Bremner, John Charles (the great one), Terry Hibbit (Leeds), John Charles (West Ham), Socrates, Bobby Robson, David Harvey, Steve (Kalamazoo) Mokone, Helen Skilbeck – Leeds Information Library, Freddie Apfel, Lucas Radebe, Andy Preece, Kester Aspden, Phil Beaver (Nottingham White), Gary Mason, Frank Bruno, Gerry Francis, Keith Walwyn, Alan Ball, Clive Middlemass, Harry Vickers, Brian Clough, John Lyall, Colin Yates, Phil Vasili, Ray Wilson, Bob Stokoe, Peter Osgood, Rodney Hinds, Keith Newton, Justin Fashanu, Pele, Sir Alf Ramsey, Alan Davies, Keith Macklin, Ron Greenwood, David Rocastle, Jimmy Baty, George Best, Robert Endeacott, Ivan Ponting, Peter Raath, Moussa Sidibe, Roy Essandoah, Manny Omoyinmi, Paul Eubanks, Harvey Marrs, Guy McKenzie, Paul Dews (LUFC press officer), also positive thanks go to the wonderful people of Germiston, Johannesburg, and the many folk from there who knew Albert and recounted dozens of thrilling tales, in particular: Benny, Joel, Kirky, Ginger, Gordon, Steel, Dangerous Darkie, Wally, Bryan, Sandy, Zebra, Flo, Dora, Jo, Benjy, Plum, Harry, Jim, Ken and Flynn. I could not produce a book such as this without mentioning the excellent message boarders on the Leeds United Mad and LUFC talk forums, we may have different names and identities but we are all from one united family. Finally, thanks must go to Karl Waddicor and his excellent publishing team at Vertical Editions for believing in the book and getting Albert's story told. If I have missed anyone, I'm sorry.

# Introduction

For many years I lived in the great northern city of Leeds, well, to be more precise it was the Crossgates, Oakwood and Garforth, areas, all have served as locations where my physical home was situated. My spiritual home, the place where I gained the vast majority of my more positive childhood and adult memories and recollections is to be found in postcode LS11. Elland Road, home of Leeds United AFC, the finest football side on the planet. It goes without saying, that living in the city I seized every opportunity to watch my beloved football team. Be they playing at home or away, I, along with thousands of other dedicated souls travelled the length and breadth of England to see them. It wasn't out of habit or misguided loyalty that I followed and supported Leeds United, it was simply because that's the way it was and it remains that way now.

Being a child of the 1960s, I lived through the greatest period of transition that Leeds United has seen. Out went the blue and gold coloured playing strip, replaced by the all white kit, complete with the wise old city owl adorning the left breast. The Leeds manager, Don Revie once said: 'If all white is good enough for Real Madrid, then it's good enough for Leeds United.' He was right too.

Like so many other youngsters of that era, I sought only a diet of football, football and more football. What a great city for a young man to live in, even better, what a superb football team to follow, my life seems inextricably linked to the club. We have both had our fair share of 'ups and downs' and in recent times things haven't been all good, yet Leeds United remains, for many of us, an absolute passion that will never fade or go away as we head for our indeterminable destination.

Throughout football, it is widely acknowledged that the late Don Revie, who replaced Jack Taylor as first team manager of Leeds United on 1 March 1961, transformed a very average, if not a struggling Leeds team, from second division also rans, to first division champions and beyond. A variety of trophies were won during what is known as the 'Revie Years'; the Second Division Championship, the Football League Championship, the Football League Cup, the Charity Shield, the European Fairs Cup (twice). Dependent upon what you read and who you listen to, Revie has been portrayed as everything from a genius, to a schemer, to a deeply superstitious and greedy man. There is currently a whole new episode of Revie revisionism occurring at the time I write this, books, magazines, articles, there is even a statue to be built in recognition of what he achieved at Leeds United. Whether such accolades are warranted is down to personal opinion. Before I started to research this book, to me Don Revie was an untouchable god, the greatest football manager of his era, a wonderful family man and a great human being. Perhaps though, I saw him through rose tinted glasses?

There are many who don't agree with the glorification of this man, professional footballers and knowledgeable football people who knew him, claim there existed 'a negative side' to his character, a side which relatively few witnessed. It seems that those who did, prefer to forget about it and won't discuss it. I first heard of such matters pertaining to Don from the late Brian Clough. However, other such nemesis of the man, such as Bob Stokoe and Alan Ball, describe him as having a difficult and often hostile personality. More of that will be revealed later. I am in no way desecrating the image of Leeds' greatest ever manager, I hold him in the highest esteem and having met him when I was a young boy, I recall how much of a giant he was, not only physically but in his presence also. Don Revie is rightly revered for what he achieved for Leeds United.

Back in the 1960s, when I was a mere child, for one reason or another, I focused much of my attention on Leeds United. It seemed to me that each game brought with it further wonders and adventures, never to be forgotten memories, especially those from very special European nights. Nights, when the huge diamond shaped floodlights of the Elland Road stadium, lit up the whole of the Leeds skyline like giant lighthouse beacons warning unwanted raiders from afar of the dangers that lurked therein. The danger being the armoury deployed in the form of the supreme skills of ten footballers wearing all white and a further one in green, as they battled and regularly outfought some of the world's greatest footballers and their respective teams. The best football sides that Europe could offer in that era came to Elland Road to do battle. Few left Leeds with any kind of positive outcome, as Leeds United marched through, and conquered Europe.

Football of the 1960s wasn't anything like as high profile across the media and public as it is today. As children and fans we had to make do with just a few football magazines – *Charles Buchan's Football Monthly*, or, *Goal*, for our regular fix of football. Within these journals, we would see close up portraits or action shots of each of our favourites: Billy Bremner, John Giles, Jack Charlton and the exotically sounding Albert Johanneson. I vividly remember thinking as a child, that a player with such a fantastic name, 'Johanneson' must be very good, my belief had to be based solely on his surname, since his Christian name had a distinctly Yorkshire and British feel to it, Albert!

What also made Albert stand apart from almost anyone in British football back then, was his colour, he was black and therefore extra special, just like Eusebio or Pele.

I was too young to determine whether I could go to football matches during the greater part of the 1960s, such decisions were generally left to my brother, or my uncle, but mainly it was down to my mother. If I had been able, I would have gone to watch football much earlier than I eventually did – I was eight when I lost my professional football spectator virginity and it wasn't even a game that included Leeds United! No, it was at the less than classic fixture between Carlisle FC and Huddersfield Town. There I caught sight of a couple of ex-Leeds players whose names I instantly recognised, Terry Caldwell and Peter McConnell. Neither seemed blessed with fantastic amounts of skill or talent, yet both were determined and tough and always seemed to do what was asked of them without making any kind of fuss. I remember my brother saying that they were, 'I will kick you into the stand if you make a fool of me' type of footballer, the kind of player that didn't mess about. They took no prisoners if they couldn't get the ball, and invariably stopped the man from getting past them. Characters of the kind that the game needs today, and to be fair to both, they did well for themselves, particularly with lower league clubs where they excelled and showed supreme loyalty and determination.

The one player that did stand out to my naive young eyes that day, was the Huddersfield Town goalkeeper, John Oldfield, he looked every bit a great keeper. With a lanky, gangly frame, he displayed an assertive presence in his goal, commanding his penalty area and I remember him constantly barking instructions at his defenders who, it seemed, obeyed his every command. Oldfield wore the attire I had seen only in pages of football magazines, a less than flattering bright green goalkeeper's jersey, with a red coloured baseball cap almost enveloping his entire head. Despite this abject display of colour coordination, the Huddersfield goalkeeper repelled every Carlisle attack. I was impressed.

Afterwards, I reflected on John Oldfield as a goalkeeper, he was good, almost as good as the greatest goalkeeper of them all, Lev Yashin. Now there was a man of immense stature, he was ultimately voted as the greatest goalkeeper of the 20th century by the International Federation of Football History and Statistics. I'm certain John Oldfield would appreciate being mentioned in the same category as Yashin if he was still around. Sadly, he passed away in 2002. To be brutally honest, the only accurate similarity between both men was that both did the same job: they were goalkeepers. There was in fact, a huge difference between the two, for a start, John Oldfield played for Huddersfield Town and was earning his corn in far less salubrious surroundings, and for that matter, against far inferior opposition to that of his Russian counterpart, who plied his trade with Dynamo Moscow. Yashin was also the Russian international first choice goalkeeper.

Lev Yashin was universally known as the 'Black Spider'. This wasn't only because he wore a distinctive all-black outfit, but rather, because he frequently pulled off the most incredible saves. One thwarted opposition centre forward described him as seemingly having eight arms, with which he could save almost everything fired at him and his goal. Fans of Dynamo Moscow often referred to him as the fearless 'Black Panther' because he defiantly commanded his penalty area and would athletically launch himself towards wherever the ball may be. Imagine then, my incredulity, as a child, when I found out that at Leeds United we had a player of our very own who had an equally exhilarating and exciting nom de plume. We had 'The Black Flash' – Albert Johanneson.

For the better part of my life, as part hobby and part professional role, I have successfully tracked down and interviewed footballers and football related people who played and featured in what I still regard as the greatest era ever in football – the 1960s and 1970s. Especially so, those of Leeds United, the team and club who have commandeered much of my focused attention, alongside my family and not forgetting my other hero, Batman. I have been extremely fortunate to meet and speak with many of football's greatest players and football related people. Don Revie was knowledgeable and, to me, seemed like a true gentleman. Billy Bremner was the best, he was like a mate you would meet and chat to in a pub – albeit I always felt in awe of him. Billy remains my all time favourite, meeting Pele in Sheffield was surreal, quite incredible really, he had a real presence, yet he was down to earth and entirely genuine. Then there was Brian Clough – despite his bluster and anger, he was a good bloke to interview. He simply said it as he saw it. Unfortunately for him, it wasn't always how it actually was, especially where Leeds United was concerned. Though in his later, 'post' managerial years, he did open up a bit more about his time at the club and seemed less hostile. Well, just a little bit anyway. George Best I always felt sympathy for. He was media exploited, he knew it of course and he thoroughly enjoyed it, and did nothing at all to prevent it. He was fine company and the last time I saw him before his sad and untimely death, he was extremely bitter about many people in the game. He felt betrayed about certain things that had happened to him during his playing days and after. George was also very open and honest about how the game was back in his playing days and I respected him for that.

Sir Bobby Robson has to be regarded as one of the greatest ambassadors of the game. Speaking with him was like being in the presence of royalty. When he spoke, you instantly believed. Lucas Radebe is another I have chatted to. The one thing I can say about Lucas is, once you meet him and spend some time with him, you are aware that you have been in the company of someone very special indeed. Over the years, I guess I have got to meet most of my Leeds' football idols, and with the sole exception of one occasion and one player, I have never felt let down by any of them. To me, they are still gods to this very day. I am proud to be able to say that I can add Albert Johanneson to the list of memorable football people I have met and, in his case, got to know. It is with some conviction that I can say that Albert was very much more than just another footballer; he was a brave and influential ambassador of the change that saw the diversification of football the world over.

It was more by fate than good judgment that I first met Albert Johanneson. Certainly, my first face to face conversation with Albert was neither contrived nor football related. We sort of accidentally happened upon each other in a Leeds city centre pub. Since the mid 1970s, every Saturday evening, I, along with a group of friends made the two hour journey into deepest and darkest Lancashire. Wigan to be exact. Wigan wasn't, and to be honest, still isn't, the most appealing town in the north of England. However, at that time (since 1973 actually) Wigan was famous for another reason – Wigan Casino – home of Northern Soul, and the legendary 'all nighter' dancing and music sessions. For the maturing Paul Harrison, weekends represented just three things: Leeds United, music and Wigan Casino. What else could a teenager want from life? Then, in 1981 that all changed. The councillors of Wigan Town Council stole from me, a major part of my life. They closed down Wigan Casino – allegedly to build a brand new Civic Centre on the site. It left thousands of us 'Northern Soulies' homeless on a Saturday night, something I have never quite been able to forgive Wigan and local politicians everywhere.

The building and its contents actually burned down before being comprehensively bulldozed from existence by the council, a short time later. From that day forth I resolved that I would allow no one to take from me, my other great passion in life – Leeds United. So it was, in 1980, that I opted to permanently mark my allegiance to the football club. I wanted something that was very definitely mine and was very personal to me. It was time for a tattoo.

At the time, the thought of displaying on my arm, a Leeds United tattoo, in such far off places as Majorca or Benidorm or Torremolinos seemed appealing. I was rightly proud to be associated with Leeds United, so for me, it was the right decision to make. In the company of a few fellow Leeds fans, I decided on which individual tattoo design I was going to have, and to aid the decision making process, along with fellows, I took a tour of the Leeds city centre pubs. Don't get me wrong, I had no intention of being tattooed while under the influence of drink. A tattoo is important, for a start it's permanent, therefore its ramifications have to be carefully considered. I knew what design I wanted. Having seen the Leeds United 'Yorkshire Rose' emblem, that was the tattoo for me. Subtle, smart and importantly, it made a statement – or so I thought anyway!

So there we were, touring Leeds city centre on a warm summer afternoon, the sun shining down upon the residents of the world's greatest city. It was bliss. Walking along Briggate, we turned into the alley that leads to the Ship public house, a fine hostelry and one of our regular city centre watering holes. There we ensconced ourselves in a quiet corner, and sat down to drink, talk, and to generally put the world to rights.

We hadn't been in the pub very long before 'it' happened. Someone standing at the bar loudly called out to a man who had just entered the premises. 'Albert, Albert, what do you want pal, a pint?' he enquired of the stranger, who was stood with his back towards us. There was nothing untoward or sinister about the matter, in fact it was the sort of incident that happens in every pub up and down the land a hundred times a day. Yet on this occasion, it seemed strangely different, significant almost. I glanced over at the stranger as I had caught him turning to glance round at us. For a second, time stood still, as I physically felt my jaw drop open in bewilderment, it took me a few moments to comprehend just who it was, but there looking directly at me, was Leeds legend Albert Johanneson. I had to do a double take because I couldn't believe that it was actually him. Reams of pointless information and data were activated and passing through my brain, as I sought in the deepest recesses of my memory, all the images I had of Albert. The man I was looking at was of the same height, though naturally, he looked a bit older and dare I say, a bit more weightier. Beneath a well worn overcoat that had clearly seen better days, he wore a shirt and tie. I confess to feeling a little sorry for him because, in this environment he looked more than a little nervous and uncomfortable.

A few moments later, a man approached the stranger and requested a couple of autographs for his family; the stranger duly obliged and signed the pieces of paper thrust at him. That was the validation I needed. It was confirmed in my mind that this person was indeed Albert Johanneson. It was quite surreal, but a few feet from where I sat, stood one of my all time idols. There was no way I was going to let an opportunity such as this pass, so without further ado I leapt from my seat and nervously approached the man who was now smiling at me. My hand was outstretched as I made eye contact and enquired, 'Excuse me, are you Albert Johanneson, 'the' Albert Johanneson?' He gripped my hand and shook it in return; it was a strong confident grip. 'Yes sir, I am he' came the reply. 'To whom am I speaking?' I introduced myself and I imagine, like a thousand others on a thousand different days before me, I explained to him that he was one of my great childhood heroes. He seemed quite embarrassed by this assertion and shuffled his feet, lowered his head and said 'Thank you Paul.'

I sensed that other people were beginning to gather round, almost all wanted to shake his hand and many requested his autographs. I graciously backed away and wished him well, reminding him what a privilege and honour it was to have met him. He nodded and smiled back at me, before greeting everyone who approached him as though they were a long lost friend. It seemed odd to me, that he didn't seem able to comprehend the sincerity of the positive comments and adulation in which he was held. Others noticed it too. 'Perhaps he is shy' was the common consensus of opinion. Returning to my seat and companions, the subject of our conversation changed, we began to discuss the great team that Albert had been such an integral part of. The team that the great Don Revie had built, Super Leeds.

Suddenly, our conversation was halted, as Albert appeared at the table. 'Excuse me gentlemen would you mind if I joined you, I think I need to sit down before my hand drops off because it has been shaken so much by the fine people in here,' he said, laughing and winking at us all. Without any hesitation, we made room for him. We sat mesmerised and spellbound, for fully two hours, as Albert Johanneson treated us to his own football recollections and anecdotes. It was one hell of a journey he led us through; an emotional roller-coaster. One minute we would be in fits of laughter, the next, we were recoiling in horror and despair as he told us some of the more sad and cruel incidents. I recall thinking at the time, what a great man Albert really was, what an absolute hero, almost like one of us, a good mate. Then, suddenly it was over, without warning he seemed agitated, it was as though he was late for an appointment and needed to be elsewhere. He rose to his feet and as magically as he had appeared, he was gone, bidding everyone a fond farewell, waving and smiling to us as he left the pub. It was one of those memorable moments everyone has in their life, a point and time which you know you will one day recount to your own children, to their children as well. For me, it was the day I first met the legendary Albert Johanneson.

Meeting Albert that day, and listening to some of the tales he regaled us with, had a positive and influencing impact upon me. He seemed like such a gentle and nice man, not at all like I had imagined, he was down to earth and could tell an interesting tale or two, yet there was something about his eyes that told me everything was not as it seemed. Yes, there was many a rumour floating about Leeds and football in general, of him losing his way in life, talk of him sleeping rough on the streets of Leeds and Bradford and seeking charity from any source. A fate that could befall any of us if the wrong circumstances dictated. However, I am not, and never have been, the sort of man who would judge someone by their material wealth or possessions, so supposition and talk about Albert's situation, whilst sad, influenced me not one iota. I wanted to find the man, the 'real Albert Johanneson'; the man who grew up in South Africa and followed his dreams; the footballer who caused such a fuss and commotion when he first signed for Leeds; the footballer who dazzled football audiences across the whole of Europe. It was learning more about that man which intrigued and interested me.

Fate again played a huge hand in my meeting Albert for a second time. It wasn't long after that original encounter that we met again, this time, for me anyway, it was in slightly more memorable surroundings. At the time I lived in Oakwood Grange Lane, Oakwood, LS8. It was (and so remains) a quiet, leafy tree-lined road that runs off

Oakwood Lane, it's actually a dead end, but only in the Highway Code sense.

One Saturday evening in 1981, I was returning home from watching Leeds at Elland Road, when I was stopped by a man I recognised as a neighbour. I didn't know him personally, but we always acknowledged one another's existence when we saw each other. He asked: 'How Leeds had got on,' before introducing himself as Harry Vickers. He said he had seen me wearing my colours (a white blue and gold scarf) and going to games every week and he thought this admirable. Harry explained how he was now retired, but at one point in his life he had been on the playing books of Leeds United. I was impressed, very impressed. Over the coming days I made it my business to get to know a bit more about Harry, he was a lovely proud man and we sat for many hours discussing the various stages of Leeds United throughout history. He had on display in his home, an impressive portrait painting of himself in an old blue and gold Leeds shirt.

Although there was several decades age difference between us, we became friends, his wife told me that since he had met me and had been reminiscing, he was like a young man again. Over many weeks Harry recounted many incredible tales of Leeds United greats of the 1920s, 1930s and 1950s, the majority were players I had read of, yet sadly, they were nothing but names to me. Then Harry began to mention football people whose names I recognised and knew of, players and people I had worshipped: Jackie Charlton, Mick Jones, Bobby Collins, Billy Bremner (who I knew), Don Revie, John Charles, Terry Cooper, Allan Clarke, Paul Reaney. I felt extremely privileged to meet and listen to Harry, and to gain such an insight to all things Leeds United and we became friends.

Later, Harry invited me to an official function at Elland Road. The venue was the social club, a gaunt looking building that stood on, and looked out across Fullerton Park training pitch. It was a meeting of the Leeds United ex-players association. What an honour to be attending such an event, especially so as I was nothing more than a supporter and never had, nor could I attain the requisite skills to play for the world's greatest football team.

My own greatest football achievement being to play for Yorkshire Amateurs in the Leeds Red Triangle League, oh, and having a trial with Preston North End, which resulted in a 'don't call us, we'll call you comment' from one of the coaches monitoring the trial. I was a left winger and in truth, I hadn't got near kicking the ball during my fifteen minute trial. I ran about a lot, chased the ball a lot, fell over a lot, shouted a lot. It just didn't happen for me, nerves and blind panic ensured that the 'headless chicken' part of my game came to the fore and was duly noted. Needless to say, I never heard another thing from Preston.

I was excited by the thought of attending an 'ex-players association' meeting, and dressed and acted in a conservative manner for the occasion, I donned a shirt and tie and shoes. I knew I had to behave and act like a grown man, not like an overawed schoolboy when meeting my heroes. My excitement must have been obvious to Harry, who reminded me as we were parking our car in the main Elland Road car park behind the West Stand, that the players were human beings like us and to remember it was a privilege for them to meet me as well as me them. As an equality speech it was rousing, sadly though it had no effect on my nervous state and didn't stop the butterflies flitting around in my stomach.

We climbed the sixteen stone steps that led up from the main car park and onto the grass-covered training ground, and walking by the ten foot tall perimeter fence we made our way to the social club. My heart skipped a beat when I saw walking in front of us, and clearly going to the same venue, Allan Clarke, Norman Hunter and Bobby Collins. The latter two, Hunter and Collins, were, at the time, the managerial duo at South Yorkshire side, Barnsley. 'Sniffer' Clarke also had associations with South Yorkshire, having been the previous manager at Barnsley, before moving to what was an unsuccessful spell at Leeds.

On entering the social club, a venue I had never before visited, I was surprised at the working men's club style decor, the dour interior decor was broken by the occasional photograph and memorabilia hanging on each of its the walls. Leeds United greats, players, managers and teams peered down at the clientele. It took me a few moments to acquaint myself with my surroundings, it was then that I saw gathered before me, not in photographs or images, but in human form, a veritable real life A to Z of Leeds United. Familiar faces of players were everywhere to be seen. I felt overawed and not at all certain that I could contain or control my excited state. Harry took me round and introduced me to each and every one of these gods, to my satisfaction, all were friendly and welcoming. I was introduced as 'his friend,' which validated my being there and gave me a feeling of being accepted by the group. Eventually, having done the rounds of introductions, we sat down at a table alongside Bobby Collins. I desperately wanted to whip out a pen and piece of paper and ask for autographs, but I realised that this would not be the accepted protocol in such auspicious company.

Glancing round, I saw sat at the next table the daunting and unforgettable figure of Jack Charlton who saw me looking over, and gave me a reassuring wink. Other people arrived after us, familiar faces were everywhere. I was like a child in a sweet shop, excited, overwhelmed and thoroughly happy. Looking around the room, sat in one corner I saw the rather forlorn looking figure of Albert Johanneson. He looked neither well, nor happy, he was sat alone and I instantly felt sympathy for him as he appeared to be extremely uncomfortable. He was staring into space, but eventually glanced over at me and raised his hand to acknowledge me, he smiled and I reciprocated. I had no idea if he recognised me or not.

The ex-players association meeting itself, whilst relaxed, had a formal agenda, indeed, to be honest, it was fairly boring to me as a first time guest. The various stages of the meeting were discussed and matters resolved and the outstanding agenda items gradually disappeared until the meeting was formally drawn to a close. Finally, it was over, then came the socialising (or networking as it is now called), a chance for these 'gods' to chat to one another and catch up on the latest adventure of each other's lives. I mingled and smiled a lot, but generally felt out of my depth, being in the company of my childhood heroes was an awesome experience and I was determined to try to take it all in.

I gradually made my way to Albert, who struck a sad figure. He was still sitting alone. My heart went out to him, he looked lost and was clearly feeling left out. It has to be said that this was more deliberate on Albert's behalf than of him being consciously ostracised or ignored by anyone in the room It seemed that he didn't want to mix and I noticed that he was drinking tap water.

I reminded him of our all too brief meeting in the 'Ship' in Leeds city centre and to my surprise he remembered the encounter. He invited to me to join him and moved a chair for me to sit down. Albert was clearly out of sorts, he looked as though he had been crying and he was acting furtively, looking around as though he had done something wrong or expected something bad to happen. I had no idea why he was behaving like this, and wondered if he was feeling unwell. I asked him if he was feeling okay. Staring at his glass, he told me he was ashamed about something that had happened; he didn't further expand upon the comment. I certainly wasn't in any position, as a mere acquaintance, to inquire the reason behind this comment but could see he was emotionally hurting. His eyes were now transfixed on the floor, occasionally darting up to meet my gaze then averting back to the ground again. It was a strained situation and I wondered if I was pressuring Albert by speaking to him, I decided to try to calm him by making small talk and explaining a bit about me and why I was at the meeting. This seemed to have the desired effect, as he became more engaging and asked me a bit about my own life. Suddenly, it all felt very comfortable, he was chatting and gave the occasional laugh as he again told me stories of his life in football.

It was at this point that I recognised that it may be pertinent to record something in writing about his life and career. I asked if I could interview him some other time, about his time in football, he said he would like that. I followed this up by asking him for a contact telephone number, only to be told that there wasn't one he could give me. I asked how I could get hold of him in the future and my heart sank like the Titanic when he told me that if I went to the Three Legs pub on the Headrow, someone there would tell me where he would be and how I could get hold of him. It all seemed a little sinister and it didn't make sense to me at all. Surely a footballing man like Albert Johanneson couldn't have been left to flounder to the point where he had no permanent address? I asked him if he was working. He smiled and explained: 'I do a bit here, and a bit there, life for me is about surviving, I do think I could still play professional football if I was given the opportunity, but I rarely have the money to pay for a bus ride from Headingley to get to the training ground, so I can't get fit, I can't afford to eat the right food and it leaves me feeling very dejected about everything.'

I was fumbling in my pocket for a few quid to give him when I became aware that Harry was beckoning me over; he wanted to leave. I surreptitiously passed Albert a tenner, and bid him and each of the remaining other gods who were present, a good night and left. I felt like the player being substituted as I walked past each of them and out of the building.

I was concerned and very sad and emotional about Albert's situation. I wanted to help him, it was obvious to me that life had got on top of him and although I did not dare utter the phrase, by the bloodshot state of his eyes, he was clearly drinking too much alcohol.

As we drove away from Elland Road and towards the city centre, I saw the plump looking figure of Albert Johanneson walking along the pavement behind the South Stand of the football stadium. Harry explained that Albert had fallen on desperately hard times, and that very evening he had received some financial support from members of the ex-players association. I felt saddened and I will never forget the awful image of Albert, wearing a long fawn coloured overcoat, with the collar turned up around his neck. His once broad and muscular shoulders were now hunched forward, as he slowly made his way along Elland Road. Once a revered footballer, he was now nothing more than a shadow in the Leeds night.

Being a football historian, I have a desire to learn more about the background and infrastructure of our great game, particularly that relating to Leeds United. Albert Johanneson is a huge part of that and I wanted to know more about the man with the exotic sounding name. The man whose image, along with countless other members of the Leeds squad of that era, had for so long adorned my bedroom wall. It became something of a personal quest for me: 'The search to find the real Albert Johanneson.' I realised from the outset that only Albert could give me such an insight, it wouldn't be easy, I had to gain his trust and importantly, I had to be able to trust in what he said to me. I also knew that it would be all too easy to be swayed by public and media opinion, and to categorise Albert in a negative manner. My search had to be focused and deliberate and truthful. So the journey began . . .

\* \* \* \* \*

Since Albert was such a well known personality in the city, unfortunately for his activities both on and off the field, it wasn't really that difficult to find him. From the people I spoke to, officials and persons of great integrity who knew Albert, I was made aware that in recent times he had attracted the 'wrong' sort of people to his life, hangers on, leeches who were abusing his football notoriety within the city. I was warned that some of these people were less than unfortunate and were most definitely not the kind of persons who could be trusted; they were negative personalities and influences on Albert's life. I was also alerted, that unlike Albert, some of them were dangerous and would do anything to keep Albert believing they were looking after his best interests.

I was feeling a little disillusioned by this information, since it was clearly in part, going to be a journey into the murky world of some of Leeds' less salubrious characters, alcoholics, drug addicts, street beggars and associated nefarious activities that would undoubtedly lead to crime and matters of crime. I constantly wondered how on earth Albert had been allowed to fall so far from grace? How had he found himself in these circumstances? Did we as a society influence his circumstances and could we have prevented it? At that point, I didn't know Albert at all well, yet I felt an overwhelming guilt that he had been let down by Leeds as a city and by us as people and communities of that city and supporters of Leeds United.

I had to strategically plan how I was going to win Albert over, gain his confidence, trust and understanding and create acceptable moral and ethical boundaries that should never be breached by either of us when in each other's company.

It was easy planning a course of action, however, the delivery was always going to be a more difficult aspect. For a start, Albert already had a network of people surrounding him, I hadn't met them, yet it was clear that these people were virtually suffocating and controlling him. He had learned routines, part of which included regular contact with that network of 'friends.' I use the latter term in the loosest possible sense. These people indoctrinated in him a false belief that he was not to trust new faces, or give out any information or interviews without one of them being there and receiving some financial compensation which undoubtedly would be split in their favour.

I considered all of the obvious perils and dangers of getting involved in research such as this, not forgetting the amount of time, work and effort the project was going to cause, and there have been many times when I felt it wasn't worth pursuing, yet something within, drove me on, and despite various and countless threats on my life, and other reckless efforts to get me to drop my research, I continued, not least because I was encouraged by Albert himself who seemed to realise the effort I was putting in was very real and for all the right and positive reasons. He told me that he wanted someone to record his life story as a legacy for his partly estranged family, especially the two great loves of his life, his daughters; Alicia and Yvonne. Whenever he spoke of his girls, his eyes sparkled, revealing the inner and real passion he felt inside for them both. His love for his ex-wife Norma was unconditional. He would often refer to her as being 'the greatest woman alive.' He felt he had let each of them down, he felt he had let the people of South Africa, Germiston and Johannesburg down, he felt he had let the people of Leeds down. He told me in 1982:

Sir, people will not want to read a book about Albert Johanneson, I am not important in this great world, people outside of Leeds and perhaps Yorkshire will not remember me. People see me as being different, I am black, they still point their fingers at me and shout horrid things, sometimes they say vile and cruel things, sometimes they pat me on the back and tell me I am a hero. I am not a hero. I am not very interesting at all. You can write the book about me, but 'you' will have to do it because no one will want to know if I write it. They see me as a nuisance, an irritating black man who is worthless and should be behind bars.

The police target me, they see me as a street beggar and not a human being, they sometimes chase me around for fun. I try to run away, but they easily catch up with me without running. They laugh at me because I'm not as quick as I used to be, and when they catch me they shoulder charge into me and tell me I am as slow as a snail. The police are not my friends, they are not culturally aware, to me they are nothing but racist bullies. If I stop to talk to people in Vicar Lane or Briggate or anywhere in the city centre, the police will turn up and tell me to move on and not to loiter and hassle people. I don't hassle anyone, it's normally people who stop me and start to talk. It's not a crime for people to stand and speak in the street, but if you are a black ex-footballer called Albert, and in Leeds, then you are targeted by the police as some kind of criminal.

Not long ago (1981), a policeman in Albion Street had words with me for sitting on the pavement, I wasn't doing anything that was wrong or illegal, I wasn't begging or being a nuisance, I was just sat down on the pavement minding my own business. I sat down because my knees were hurting. The policeman grabbed hold of me by my collar and dragged me to my feet. He was rough and seemed very angry and punched me in the ribs. When I stood up he bent down and looked into my face. He told me to go away, to clear off. He said that no one wanted me or my sort in Leeds, and that I should go back to live with all the other darkies in Africa, either that, or I should be locked away behind bars, either in a prison, or in a zoo.

It's disgraceful. I went to report that to the police at Millgarth, to make a complaint, they laughed at me and told me I was an old drunk, and to crawl back under the stone from where I came. It's upsetting, frustrating, not having a voice and not being listened to or believed, especially when it is the law that is committing the crime, then denying it. That's how most people see me, they don't really want me here, I am something to be stared at, pitied, a nobody, a nothing. What I suffered and saw in South Africa in my youth was no different in the hurtful torment and pain I suffer here. The police are as corrupt and society doesn't really want to know the truth.

I asked Albert who he was referring to when he said, 'they.' He made it very clear that he meant the faceless authorities of local and central government. At such an early stage of our friendship, it was difficult to put matters in perspective for Albert, I offered my reassurance and told him how unacceptable and abhorrent I found such behaviour and how most other reasonable people would view it as that too. I did my best to convince him that not all police officers were bad, but as in all professions, (I knew from personal experience that the police were not exempt) there exists a rogue element. Spineless people in authority who abuse and hide behind their positions and feel themselves above criticism and in many cases, that included government bodies and the law. Such words or opinions mattered little to Albert, the damage had been done long ago.

Its happened a lot, that wasn't a one-off with the police.

I have problems with them mocking me, maybe once or twice a week. No matter how much I protest, they just laugh and call me names, some openly try to aggravate me, hoping for a violent or vitriolic response so they can make an arrest and lock me up for the night. Other people's lives are nothing but a stupid game for them.

For Albert, no amount of sympathy or rational opinion could begin to eliminate or erase the memory of a lifetime of continually being treated as different. I felt upset that he had been treated so abhorrently and that this once brave and handsome sportsman should suffer as much as he clearly had. I wished I could right the wrongs and injustices Albert had endured throughout his life. My emotions got the better of me and I felt a tear trickle down my cheek and I found myself apologising to him for the sins of other human beings. Albert put his arm round my shoulder and gave me a hug.

I do like you Paul, you are a good man, a caring, decent and honest man, you seek nothing from me, and I seek nothing from you. I do believe you see us as equals, I respect that in you. But you must understand that there are many who don't see me like that, they cannot accept or embrace my presence as you do, they have made me into who, or what, I now am. Please forgive me if I am bitter and angered in what I say to you, it hurts when you are abused day and night, when you are struggling with everyday life, and people, complete strangers, kick, punch and spit on you, and call you offensive racist names that don't belong here today.

\* \* \* \* \*

When I was with Albert, we didn't ever share a hardened drinking session together, I respected him far too much to allow that happen. He knew that too, and I like to think that in his own way he respected me for making him abstain, at least during the time when he was with me. It wasn't always easy being in Albert's company, the lifetime of pain and abuse he had witnessed and suffered had made him cynical of everything and everyone. It was the alcohol which numbed this pain, alcohol that was openly provided by people who recognised him as one of their Leeds United idols and wanted to open the arm of friendship to him. Sadly, they didn't know or understand that by providing him with a pint, or a short, they were causing him further pain.

When the effects of the alcohol wore off, that was when he felt low and the negative recollection of his life came flooding back, immersing him in an all-consuming ocean of gloom. I was with him during such periods, and he did at times speak offensively to me, cursing at me and questioning my integrity and failure to really understand how much pain and anguish he had suffered in his life. It took much strength and forgiveness to ignore his often acidic comments, however, I knew that when this did happen, it wasn't the real Albert who was speaking; it was his inner demons.

Generally, such issues arose when he was feeling vulnerable and frightened. The one thing he consistently did when he had acted out of sorts with me, was to apologise profusely for his out of order behaviour. After such events he would show real remorse and continually apologise for acting as he had. We would put such issues behind us with a masculine hug, and move on. I genuinely believe that throughout the time I spent in his company, we were honest with each other and he tried to recall his life, as hurtful as that often was, the best he could, albeit all too often his recollections aroused emotions that appeared to overwhelm him.

Sometimes, we would walk and talk, though he would

often complain about the pain in his knees. This was caused by countless football related injuries, and as a result of brutality he encountered on the football pitches across England. I don't deny, that at times he would only sit and talk when there was a glass of cider, or perhaps two, involved, but that's all it ever was when he was in my company: two half pint glasses maximum. He would joke with me when I bought him an orange juice or a non-alcoholic fizzy drink, telling me I needed to loosen up, relax and let myself go occasionally!

To be honest, I rarely saw him lose his temper with others and in the main, Albert was an intelligent, personable and inoffensive man. A good example of this was when he recalled one instance of someone stealing his wallet from his coat pocket, as he slept on a park bench one afternoon:

> Their need must have been greater than mine for them to steal from me. People do the strangest things when under duress; no one is without secrets, or without blame, for matters of great negativity and such things in their life. People do the craziest things. Look at me and you have proof of that.

Albert had a certain way about him, he was the type of man you could listen to, learned almost, with an ability to recount his life in a gripping and emotional manner. I would defy anyone to feel emotionally detached when they listened to recollections of his life. Despite everything, he never felt that he was a victim. He saw his life as a journey, physical and spiritual.

I feel honoured and fortunate enough to have been able to document much of Albert's journey. I can still see him now, checking over the copious amounts of handwritten notes diligently recorded by me during our interviews and meetings. He would complain about how my handwriting started very neatly then deteriorated as we progressed through each meeting. Very often he would deliberately correct the frantically scribbled notes, putting a line through words of no consequence and laughing. That was the kind of relationship we had, we both knew and understood what was important in each other's lives.

I am not certain whether it is a privilege, an honour, or I am blighted and damned, for being widely regarded as the last person to interview Albert in September 1995, just days before his sad and untimely passing. Personally, I have found the matter to be rather distressing. I later went through a period in my life, wondering whether I could have done more to help him, and so prevented his premature demise from this world. Realistically, I know that there was nothing more that I, or other friends and people who cared for him, could have done. Albert often reaffirmed:

> We are all blessed to be placed here in this life, on this earth. We each have a role to fulfill, once we have attained what our creator desires, our time to move on will come. When your time is up there is little or nothing you can do about it. Embrace each day as though it is your first, never stop believing, never stop loving and always give of your best in all you do.

On learning of his death, it felt like a huge part of me had been taken away. I feel both fortunate and proud to be able to say that I knew him, and I confess, looking back, I thoroughly enjoyed every moment of his company, sharing and listening to his stories, the good, the bad and the plain ugly.

It pains me as a biographer to state that he suffered some disturbing behaviour, both physical and verbal, the vast majority was as a result of him being black, however. Much was focused on him because he was a professional footballer, not just any kind of footballer, a quick and skilful one, and that, in part, is why he was targeted for abuse by opposition managers, players and fans alike.

Anyone seeking any kind of moralistic message as to the difficulties and pressures of fame and alcohol from this volume may as well return it to the shelf now. This book isn't about sending out subliminal messages about the perils of alcohol, or a historical review of life on the streets of the world's greatest city. It's about people, about truth, honesty and integrity; it's about chasing and living a realistic dream. This is the story of a proud man, a son, a brother, a husband, a father, an uncle, a friend. It's about Albert Louis Johanneson, a man with magic in his feet and love in his heart. A man who could be seen waltzing around the dance floors of West Yorkshire, a man who could be seen waltzing with a ball at his feet and leaving some of the world's best professional footballers in his wake. At times the language may seem strong, it is recorded here as it was said, it isn't there to shock, it was dictated with real emotion and passion, and just occasionally Albert recounted incidents with some venom.

Without Albert Johanneson, world football may not be as it is today; the Leeds United success story of the 1960s would not have been as exciting. On his day, he could transform the ugliest and dreariest of gloomy Yorkshire days into a much brighter place as he raced at defenders, putting them on their backsides or leaving them behind, always with a beaming and very proud smile on his face. Had it not been for Albert, South African, indeed, overseas footballers may never have been tempted to come to these or other European shores. Albert was a trailblazer, an ambassador, and to many a true and genuine legend.

Paul Harrison

# 1

# In the Mood

I still recall the moment when I asked Albert where it all began and to tell me the story of his South African roots. We were sat in The Albion, on Armley Road, then an everyday pub that was recognised more for its location and view – it overlooks one of Leeds' most sinister and infamous buildings, Armley Prison – than for reasons of sustenance. It was hot outside, summertime, the sun was shining and the world (Leeds in particular) was a great place to be.

Albert had been his usual chirpy, dare I say 'cheeky' self. He was wonderful to be around when he was like this, full of laughs and self confidence. His memory may not have been all it could have been, but there were good reasons for that. Too many commentators have called into questions Albert's sobriety, turning him into an infamous drunk as opposed to a human being with memories and recollections, many of which he would rather forget.

> South Africa is a great country, I am very proud of my family and my heritage, but there are things that are best left unsaid, unspoken, memories of hurt, pain and death, murder even.

Pointing out towards Armley Prison he continued:

> Many of those people in there, they are murderers, killers, rapists, ruthless evil people who deserve to be, and should be, locked out of harm's way, it is safer for them and for us as human beings that they remain locked behind bars.

I don't believe in the 'eye for an eye' style of retribution, I prefer to think that mankind has goodness within it, I like to see the best in people, until they prove otherwise.

Some of the things I saw and witnessed in the early part of my life are far worse than anything those criminals locked away in that prison could ever do, or even think of doing. Sometimes, I lay awake at night and I still see the tortured faces of little children, women and the vulnerable, each one struggling to come to terms with the inhuman actions of political abuse and sadistic domination over an entire race. Etched into their faces are vivid scenes of death, in their minds, the screams and desperate pleading of hundreds of suffering souls being tortured and in the throes of death echo like church bells ringing out. People begging to be put death, many partly mutilated in acts of real savagery by the oppressors. The pain of life for these good and innocent people was now far too great. None were ever shown mercy, they were of course left to die a painful, humiliating and slow death before their friends and family.

Sometimes, South Africa could be hell, other times, it was the greatest, most wonderful place to be. We blacks were united, as one almost. There was a universal mistrust of the white man or woman, few showed us any compassion, those that did suffered misfortune themselves. Life was a daily bout of survival and learning techniques to enable that. For example, running. If you could run like the wind, you had more chance of escaping the white oppressors.

This was an eloquent Albert Johanneson, a side of him rarely, if ever, remembered. They are the thoughts of a man who as a mere child had witnessed much more of life (and death) than the majority of us will ever encounter.

As remiss as it was of me, the one thing I never confirmed with Albert, was his date of birth. To this day it remains something of a contentious matter. My own notes, recorded at the time of my interviews with him, dictate that he told me he was born in Germiston, near Johannesburg, in South Africa's Witwatersrand region on Wednesday, the 13th March 1940. Albert's date of birth appears on his gravestone as 13th March 1942. This later date is based upon the testimony of Albert's brother Trevor, with whom he lived for a time in Leeds, and it was he who formally registered Albert's death, recording 1942 as his year of birth. Yet other records, including football league player registration documents, and the age recorded by Albert himself on his marriage certificate dictate that he was born in 1940.

It has to be said the earlier date has much more provenance than the latter, since he told me himself that he was born in 1940, and the registered date on his marriage certificate was made when his recollections were much more vivid and clear, and he was still young and with a good memory.

Despite countless searches of South African records, there is nothing that confirms the matter. Records held and maintained in that country dating back to the pre-1960 era, can be described as, scant at best. Certainly, the families of black communities were mainly anonymous (deliberately politically and socially ignored) sections of the population, that is until they required government sanctions for formal documentation, such as pass books and other items of identification to help them move about and, or, leave the country. In the main, such paperwork was for adults only, so the date and precise location of birth was down to family recollections and word of mouth.

Unfortunately, Albert's date of birth remains one of many unnecessary enigmas associated with him. Original details that have been wrongly recorded and the myth further perpetuated in the writings of countless writers and journalists over the years. Eventually, those myths become accepted fact. Hopefully, with the publication of this work, many of these misnomers will now be corrected and laid to rest.

It is worth pointing out at this stage, that Albert was passionate about music and dancing, curiously, this often reflected his frame of mind and we often discussed the different types of music. It is therefore poignant that topping the music charts when he was born in 1940, was Glenn Miller's *In the Mood*. Certainly from a footballing perspective, Albert's on the pitch performances very much depended upon whether he was in the mood. Where possible, because it's what Albert would have wanted, I have attempted to incorporate some of the music titles of note from the era, that impacted upon the various phases of his life and nationally popular at the time.

South Africa in the 1940s was a highly political and hostile environment, formally culminating in apartheid in 1948. However, long before that time it had been a land of confrontation and oppression beginning in the mid-17th century. History records that white settlers, originally from the Netherlands came to the country, and seized control from black resident and occupants of townships, literally driving them from their homes, off their land and forcing them into an almost nomadic lifestyle. Many remained in situ and were used as labourers to the white folk, sleeping outdoors and surviving off discarded scraps of food. Labourers of course, was nothing but a political term, the reality of the situation was, the black people were used as slaves.

During the following two centuries it seemed that most of Europe wanted a piece of Africa, and what has been termed as the 'Scramble for Africa' occurred as the Belgians, British, Dutch, French, Germans, Portuguese and Spanish, took control of most of the fifty states consisting in the entire African nation. As far as Southern Africa is concerned, it was separated into four separate territories towards the end of the 19th century, two being under British rule and control (the Cape Colony and the Colony of Natal), whereas the remaining two (South African Republic and the Orange Free State) were the territory of the Afrikaners. Not that this helped the black people of the country, they held no rights whatsoever; they had no political rights in any of the four territories, and therefore no voice and no positive future. Segregation and exclusion was clearly evident and in full flow by this stage.

The constant battle for supremacy and power continued across South Africa, British rule was overwhelming and all-consuming. Descendants of the original 17th century Dutch settlers, who were also referred to as Boers or Afrikaners, felt the British to be subjective and dismissive of their existence. It was a tense, hostile and fragmented environment. Culminating with the Boers revolting against the British, so began the Anglo-Boer war of 1899–1902, as each battled it out in an attempt to claim control of the two other colonies. The British fought off the challenge, and British rule was so established across all four colonies. The two independent colonies were renamed, being titled the Transvaal Colony and the Orange River Colony respectively. After various conventions and constitutions, a Bill was formally passed by British Parliament on 20 September 1909. On the same date, King Edward VII proclaimed that the Union of South Africa was to be established and formed on 31 May 1910. This effectively joined the four colonies together, with the British relinquishing the entire administration of the country to white local people.

Once again, the black population was ignored, denied any voice or opinion. Somewhat shamefully, the new union preserved all ruling and restrictive regulations on black rights. It also removed all parliamentary rights for black people across South Africa.

The South Africa Albert Johanneson was born into was unfamiliar to that seen across Britain of the same era, indeed, it couldn't be more different. Racial segregation existed everywhere, the white domination was prevalent across all aspects of society. Socially, there was no interaction or integration; property and land ownership was biased towards the white people, the legal system was virtually non-existent if you were black, and all importantly as a result of the social economic situation, the distribution of wealth was extremely biased in favour of the white people.

My parents (Louis and Caroline Johanneson) were really good people, with good intentions and very hard working. They were different in many ways, dad was a mechanic and very protective of us all. He was a proud man who always put his family before himself. He provided for us. He taught us the ways of the street, whereas mum taught the family – I had brothers and a sister – the importance of unity and caring.

My earliest childhood memories of life in the townships around Johannesburg and the Transvaal area has been clouded by so many different, difficult to understand incidents. As a child you have an innocence that lasts until you are introduced to society and the peculiar ways of whichever society you belong to. That's when you become influenced by adults, and that dictates the way you act and reflects within your morals and beliefs as you grow through adolescence and into adulthood.

I grew up officially before apartheid (1948). As a little boy I had no idea or understanding of what it meant, it was indoctrinated into us as children, that black people are inferior to whites. I must have been four or five years old before I physically saw a white child of the same age as me. I could only briefly glance at him, I wasn't allowed to speak or acknowledge his existence in any way. He passed me on a street corner as he was sat in the back of a big car which had no roof, that had been folded away.

As I played with my friends, the car slowed down to a standstill, right next to us. No one spoke. I recall there being a dreadful and intimidating atmosphere. My friends stood motionless, like statues, staring at the ground. I was closest to the car. I saw out the corner of my eye the boy leaning forward towards me, then I felt his spit running down the side of my face. I did not move to wipe it off. He spat on me again and was giggling. A man stood up, he was in the rear of the car too. I was waiting for more spit, but was shocked when he produced something like a long horse whip and whipped me across the back of my neck. Instantly, I fell to the floor, not through the hurt or pain, but in an attempt to protect myself from further attack.

As I lay on the dusty road, I felt the blood running from the wound, down my neck and onto the ground. The man called for me to stand up. I didn't, I lay there frightened, terrified. The white man got out of the car. I then saw my friends run for their lives. The man came to where I lay, he stood beside me and demanded I get up. I lay still. He told me I should be butchered for daring to stand in the way of their car. He then kicked me in the face with his shiny right boot and left me laid there. I was so relieved when he got back into the car and it drove off. I jumped up and ran as fast as my legs would carry me. I didn't want to go home in the state I was, it would have been too upsetting for my family to see me like that. Even at such a young age I wanted to show them I was able to look after myself. So I cleaned myself up with water from a land container.

It was a truly terrible thing, no matter how people try to justify it. No set of human beings has the right to treat another like we 'blacks' and 'coloureds' as they called us and those of mixed race, suffered in South Africa at the hands of the white people. We couldn't walk on the same streets as them, speak to them, shop in the same stores, or live and go to the same areas where they lived or visited. As young children we were soft targets and were punished if we dared to breathe the same air as white people: it was that ridiculous. We had coloured schools and there was absolutely no integration or mixing with white families allowed, it still makes me very sad now to reflect upon it all.

To be honest, the schooling wasn't what people envisage it to be, there wasn't any real structure to our education. The teachers though, were the best, they really did work with us as individuals and as groups of children. As part of school in a township you were made to feel part of something unique, a special family. It was an all black family. It was here that you learned the terrible ways of the white world beyond South Africa. We heard of wars and aeroplanes dropping bombs and white man fighting with white man for the sake of supremacy and control. It sounded like an awful world, yet I often wondered if it could be any worse than that in which I lived.

The sad thing was, we, as a race of people, knew no different, this was our world. We knew nothing of living in harmony with others with a different coloured skin who, it seemed, held totally different beliefs to us, the main one being, that we, as black people, were not worthy.

Fighting, confrontation and war were everyday facts of life. To us, our whole existence was about living on the edge, survival, and watching out for the warning signs of the white man's anger, or even retribution from our own kind with gang fighting.

While we, the black communities, were one big family, it would be easy for me to say that we worked and lived together in harmony. I wasn't oblivious to the real hell that existed throughout the deprived black districts of Germiston and Johannesburg, black gangs and black on black fighting was a frequent occurrence.

In some of the busier areas in the central region there was the tall sky scraper-like buildings, the sort you would see in any busy city or economic centre. Once you moved away from that zone however, things got pretty bad, especially in the specifically designated all black areas. Here you found many homes that were little more than dilapidated garden sheds, they were usually made of wood and had corrugated iron roofs. Rarely did they have glass or protection in the windows, just old sheets or old carpets hanging there. Despite everything else that was going on around us, we generally respected one another's homes, it was a personal sanctuary for those who lived there, a place where they could forget the perils and tortures that everyday life often threw at them and existed beyond whatever the four walls were constructed of.

My own circumstances were like many others, my parents were hard working and generally kept themselves to themselves; this was the best and only way to survive. It was almost like they wanted to be invisible, unnoticed, and therefore out of danger and harm's way. I can understand why they maintained their own counsel, if news got out that you had come into any money or acquired something of value, you would often be paid an unwanted visit by rogues seeking to take it from you.

My father worked hard repairing old cars and carrying out bodywork modifications and respraying them. Generally speaking, the cars were old bangers and he did what he could to keep those who owned them, on the road. He was useful with his hands, a real master of many trades, he could create an intricate toy car or aeroplane from a block of wood or transform it into a useful household tool.

Where cars were concerned, he knew instinctively what was wrong with any car once he could hear it. He often said they (the cars) spoke to him through their engines and that's why he understood how to fix or repair them. I was really confused by this fact as a child, as I always believed that he meant they physically spoke to him. It was many years later before I realised that he meant the engine sound was the talking; he could tell from those noises, where, and why, they were unwell.

It was predominantly black people's cars he worked on, rarely the white people's, although on many occasions I do remember white people coming to him and demanding him to repair their vehicles. He would go out and buy parts and fit them, only for those same folk not to pay him. Some of them would openly steal other things, like car parts from the garage and, some even beat him and stole money from him.

As a black child, the white communities had no time for you; they saw you as a necessary evil to be bullied and maligned, an object for abuse and nothing more. I would often help my father in the garage, pretending to be a mechanic or to drive the cars that came in for repair. Whenever a white person came, my father would completely change his attitude and demeanour. He became defensive and wary. Whenever he saw a strange car pull up outside or nearby, he would take hold of me and hide me behind a pile of old car doors that he used for spare parts. These stood at the rear of the garage, where, I would crouch in frightened silence, peeking out to look at what was taking place in the garage with my father. It was our very private and personal secret, though not one I enjoyed, since being put there often meant that trouble and problems were about to happen.

On one occasion, I saw two white men walk into the garage. No words were exchanged. My father asked them what it was they wanted. The men approached him and without any provocation, they attacked him, punching him to the floor. It was terrifying to watch these violent and very angry strangers beating my father. I desperately wanted to do something to stop it, to help him, but I knew I couldn't. If they knew I was there and had witnessed what they were doing they would take me away and kill me. My father once told me that these people were government officials and the police

It wasn't rare for something like this to happen. To be honest, I witnessed it quite a few times, not only with my father but with other black people too. Sometimes when my father suffered, he would lay unconscious on the floor, not moving as they went through his belongings, taking whatever they liked. These weren't young white people or tearaways as you would probably expect. No, they were smartly dressed, older, middle aged people, which is why I believed he was right when he said they were government officials or the police. They always had a weapon, usually an iron bar to dish out the initial beating. Once dad was on the ground, they would kick him and call him terrible names. I would be in tears but had to wait until they had gone before coming out of hiding and tending to his wounds, and helping clean him up and get him sorted. He was a very proud man, he never wanted mum or anyone else to know or see him in such a state. It was our secret, or at least he thought it was. Mum knew exactly what was going on, but wouldn't ever speak out as she felt it would humiliate and embarrass him.

Life was tough for all black people in South Africa. I can look back now and see there was so much hatred and antagonism everywhere. We were forced to act subserviently and let the whites think they were superior and acknowledge our inferiority to them in every way, even though we were all the same really. It was idiotic. We were never given credit for having any intelligence or reasonable decision making ability, the only thing most believed we were capable of was labouring tasks and menial work such as backbreaking work in the mines, where people would be whipped if they stopped or slowed down. I know it's a much used saying, but animals were treated better and often had a superior lifestyle to the black community.

One of the most fearful aspects of life as a youngster in South Africa, was the fact that if anyone dared stand up to the white oppressors they suffered serious consequences. There was one time when I was about eight or nine-years-old. I had a friend, Archie, who lived close to me in our township and we would often hang out together. Archie's father was a fine man called Scott, he was what was referred to as a cobbler. He made and repaired shoes and boots and he was very good at it too. Such was his reputation that people came from many townships to have shoes repaired or made for them. Not that shoes were an everyday object, most of us had no need for them and would be barefoot day and night.

I would often go to play in Archie's district and he would come to mine. There was a group of us, we were normal young boys with an inquisitive nature and enquiring minds so we often got up to a bit of innocent mischief: smoking drugs, drinking, that kind of thing.

One afternoon, two white men visited Archie's father. They asked him to repair some shoes there and then. He couldn't do it, it was a skilled and time consuming job and he had a list of other jobs lined up. They demanded he did as they instructed and told him they were a priority. He politely explained that he couldn't do it and asked if they would come back the next day when he would be able to help them. It was not accepted protocol to say, 'No' to a white person. The men beat him with a metal pole, then stole all his money from his pocket and took several pair of shoes off him too. He was badly beaten and from all accounts, they left him in a very bad way with broken bones and hands, meaning he would not be able to work until the injuries healed.

Some other people from the township had seen the incident unfold, they knew who the men were. Thugs who were regarded as regular tyrants in the district. So the black community came out to help and stop the attack. There was much shouting and pushing as the group surrounded the two white men. Then, without any warning, one of the two pulled a gun from his coat pocket, and fired it above the heads of the mob who had gathered around them. The two whites were frightened and backed off as they believed they were going to be overwhelmed by the throng. They ran away to their car, and fled the area.

Archie's father was taken into his house and given basic medical attention and treatment. He was unable to walk, lift his head or use his hands. I remember Archie telling me that he was scared because he thought his father was going to die. I tried to reassure him that his father was a strong man, and told him that everything would be okay and not to worry about things over which he had no control. I even told him that he could come and live with my family if he wanted to. It was a terrible time because everyone, even us as children, realised that this wasn't going to be the end of the matter and that retribution would follow. There was no way that black people from the township could win or achieve any kind of victory over a white man.

Sure enough, that very same night, the whites came back in their numbers with one specific aim in mind: to kill. It mattered little who. They simply wanted blood and of course revenge. Archie and his entire family disappeared that night. I never ever saw him or them again. It was so upsetting and there was a lot of talk about what had happened. I later learned that the whole family (father, mother, three daughters and two sons including Archie) had been forcibly removed from their home, driven off to some waste ground, where they were individually tortured (the women were raped) and then executed. Seven members of one family gone, murdered, and for what?

It was a painful life and existence, a cruel, harsh world where you had to quickly adapt to your surroundings, either that, or you went under. The killing (it was murder) of Archie's family really damaged the community, more so than any other killing I can remember. It was my first real taste of loss and I didn't like it. I hated the thought of all the fighting and people losing family and loved ones. Within a week I witnessed my first ever killing of a white man and, I must add that death, destruction and killing is not something I would ever advocate, yet sometimes back in those times, well, it was just the way it had to be.

The man in question, had, over a period of time, been sexually working his way through some of the young black girls, 14 to 18-year-olds of the township, raping them and forcing them into committing dreadful acts on him. It was the ultimate in power and control, hurting us and keeping us downtrodden and scared of life on the streets. The only options available to us, were to either put up with it, or deal with it ourselves. Hand out our own form of justice. The police did not want to know, nor did they care, they would do nothing to hurt one of their own, or the white people.

On the evening in question I saw the man pull up his car in a quiet street, he got out and literally snatched a girl from the street. He kidnapped her; she screamed out in terror. The act was seen by two young men who tried to intervene but they found themselves threatened by him. He was brandishing a gun. He drove off with the girl, not far, just to a quiet and unobtrusive area where he thought he would be undisturbed. Not that he cared, he never felt threatened or intimidated by the black people. What he didn't realise was the fact that the alarm had been raised, word had spread quickly as to his actions and the community was on the lookout for him and the car.

It wasn't long before he was spotted pulling the car onto some waste ground. Within moments, a group of young black men stealthily gathered. These weren't young boys, they were hardened gang members who knew the area, knew their prey, and knew how to defend their own territory.

The white man got out of his car and forced the girl to strip naked, throwing her clothes away in random directions before pushing her into the back seat where, he began to rape her. Thankfully, he didn't get very far. Silently, like shadows in the night, the group of men surrounded the car and peered into the windows. It looked for all the world as though it was a carefully rehearsed move, with real precision and timing. The reality was different, the group was acting on nothing more than gut instinct. A few moments later the car door was pulled open and the man dragged outside. The girl was freed, her clothes recovered and she dressed before being taken away to her home.

The white man was surrounded by the group. He

was stripped naked and whipped all over. I could hear his screams and pleas for mercy, he cried like a small baby, yet not once did he say he was sorry. The group systematically whipped every part of his body with sticks, until it seemed that blood poured from every inch of skin, and every bone in his body must be broken. The bonnet of his car was then covered in petrol, the rapist was bound to it and was himself doused in petrol. This was ignited by a flame from a match, and within moments the whole bonnet area of the car burst into a huge ball of flame. Fierce at first, it soon calmed down to a slow continuous burning. It was a torturous death. He screamed and yelled and knowing his fate was sealed, continued to hurl abuse at the black people. Of course no one heard his screams, if they did, no one sufficiently cared to help or bother.

Afterwards, the car and his remains were towed away and dumped well away from the area and back in the white district as a reminder that total control was not yet achieved.

The police swamped the area for several days that followed. When I say police, back then the police were not what you could refer to as British police. The vast majority were nothing more than paid killers, sadists, military-like in appearance and attitude. They took great satisfaction in inflicting unnecessary pain on the black community as and when they saw fit, all in the name of the law. They never brought the killers of the white youth to justice, nor did they get close, albeit there was no justice in the human segregation within South Africa. Retribution was ruthless and swift, as eleven black family members were butchered or disappeared in the space of a week. It was a vicious circle with no winners.

Violence and crime was an everyday occurrence and it is only fair to say that it wasn't always white on black or vice versa. Sometimes, due to the stress and pressures of life and for reasons of self preservation and survival, tensions spilled over within communities. Inter family wars would emerge, demonstrating itself by a full blown street battle.

It always seemed to me, that when something like this happened, there was a gathered crowd of white people watching and waiting, urging the fight on, before firing off a few rounds from a pistol or rifle. Many times they fired directly into the brawling throng. People died, more often than not, innocent people. The internal fighting did nothing but feed the white man's ego that he was superior to the blacks.

It wasn't only the white men who were violent and abusive, it was something that women positively engaged in too. Once when I was about seven or eight, I strayed too far out of our territory. I found myself on the edges of a white community. I was confronted by a well dressed white woman; experience had taught me to keep my eyes fixed firmly on the ground by my feet. I stepped out of her way and tried to cross the road. She called out to me, 'Nigger boy, nigger boy, come here I want to speak to you.' Mistakenly, I looked up and she beckoned me over. I was naive and did as I was instructed. Once in front of the woman, she slapped my face so hard that I was knocked from my feet. She then kicked me as I lay on the floor, and like so many other white people in the region, she expressed her disdain and animosity towards me by spitting in my face. She grabbed hold of me by my ears and lifted me to my feet, coldly telling me she should kill me for daring to breathe the same air as she was. I was petrified and it's something I could not forget, no woman had done this type of thing to me before. I had never seen a woman act like this before with a child.

Despite everything, I was very angry with myself for foolishly straying, it was almost accepted that if you were caught even a few yards out of your area, then you would be punished. A friend, 'Dodgy Dick' had his dog shot dead because it ran into a white area. It was almost as though there were sharpshooters in waiting for any kind of incursion onto their land or territory. The dog's carcass, entirely stripped of its skin, was found back in the township area within an hour of it straying. It was a horrific existence and you truly understood the importance of keeping yourself to yourself, trusting and believing only your own family. This is why my own family did just that, all they wanted was a peaceful and safe existence for us all to live in.

It may sound ignorant, but there was no knowledge beyond that of our own townships. I knew about the war taking place in Europe, but Europe was some far off land, a place I could only imagine. It was a place I did not understand or even want to know of. My entire life consisted of my family and friends.

I began running when I was about six, to be honest. It was something you learned very quickly, since it was one of the fundamental basics of survival: running for your life. It was all barefoot, there was no such thing available to us as a training shoe or a running track. I lost the number of times I sliced open the soles of my feet on broken glass, or stubbed a toe on a rock. You just cleaned yourself up and got on with it. We would have running races among my friends and in the schools, I ran like the wind. It made me feel free, unchained, almost like I was flying like a bird. I generally won when I raced and, though it was great to be regarded as fast, it wasn't exactly something I could do to earn money to help the family.

One of the greatest motivators in my childhood running days was fear. Not fear of anything physical or human, but of more supernatural forces. As children when darkness fell we would entertain ourselves with frightening talk based upon spirits and magic. There was one tale in particular, a true story that terrified me. I can recall it as though I was told it yesterday. It was of an evil woman who lived in Germiston, she had murdered two husbands and her son. The woman was a nurse called Daisy de Melker and she poisoned both of her husbands with strychnine, and later her son with arsenic, all for money. There was much more to it than that though. She was a devious woman who practised murder for many years.

Her first paramour was a civil servant, working for the Native Affairs Department at Broken Hill. He died of Blackwater fever (a complication of malaria) on the day they were supposed to be married. Daisy was at his bedside when he passed away.

Two years later she married a plumber, William Cowle. They had five children, four of whom died! Cowle died in excruciating pain caused by the strychnine, and one doctor was suspicious of the death but was overruled in his thoughts, after a post mortem examination claimed death by more natural causes. Four years later, her second husband, a plumber called Robert Sproat, died in a similarly agonising way.

A few years later, she married again, another plumber, this time he was called Sydney de Melker. The remaining son from her first marriage, Rhodes Cecil Cowle, lived with her and her new husband, that is, until he fell ill and died just over a year after the couple had married. Now suspicions were aroused and Daisy was arrested and charged with the murder of her two husbands and her son! She was tried on all three counts, but convicted of just one count, that of her son, so Daisy was hanged by the neck. It didn't end there, the souls of her victims were said to wander around Germiston, lost, and without the ability to move on. It was said they persecute Daisy by constantly following her spirit everywhere, accompanied by their agonising cries of pain and distress, their blue faces gnarled up and distorted by the pain they still feel.

It wasn't a nice story and I confess, I never once saw the spirit of Daisy, or the family she murdered, yet plenty of others did make such claims. After dark when I was walking through the streets alone, I swear I could hear the cries of pain. That's when I ran, and you know what, despite my speed, the moment I stopped, usually when I got home, I could still hear those cries and the wailing. Daisy was like the bogeyman to me and my friends, we were terrified of her. Even though she had been dead for well over twenty years, her evil spirit seemed to be lurking around every corner, especially once darkness fell. So to be able to run fast and quickly was something I was good at, no way was that woman's spirit going to get hold of me.

It may have been a 'tongue in cheek' comment, but the fact that Albert recalled it in the first place makes it seem likely that it did have a negative impact on him, the tone of his voice and the look on his face told me that the thoughts he still had about Daisy and her victims were anything but fond memories of Germiston. The one thing that Albert hadn't mentioned of his formative years in South Africa was football. It was something that required much in the way of probing, but even then, it clearly wasn't something that greatly influenced his early years, unlike the political disharmony that surrounded him.

Football wasn't something that I was really keen on, it was primarily a white man's game. When we did go to watch, the stadium was segregated, not home and away supporters, but black and white supporters. The white spectator areas consisted of roof-covered stands, bench seats and toilets.

At Germiston Callies for instance, it was cheaper to go in to watch football as a white person. The all black areas consisted of rough banking that imitated terracing. There were no toilets, no covered accommodation; it was everything the white area wasn't. There was often a police presence in the black area, and anyone expressing an opinion would very often find themselves taken outside and brutally beaten.

It wasn't the environment you expect it to be as it is in Leeds or anywhere in England. The white sections would continually hurl abuse at the black sections, whereas we were not permitted to be vocal at all. There were always reports of white people throwing human excrement into the black area. Football hooliganism has supposedly hit epidemic proportions over here, yet it is mild and nothing compared to that in South Africa.

Back in the late 1940s and early 1950s I recall seeing pitch battles, well human slaughter really. This would occur outside football stadiums. Whites were armed and would ambush and beat black supporters leaving the ground, subjecting them to torture. The police were proactive in dishing out beatings and organising the black ambush. They would surround a group of black people, contain them and expose their vulnerability to attack from the white people.

Watching football allowed many suppressed blacks to dream of a better life, the players we watched were all white, they seemed to lead a better life and were given everything to keep them happy. Some of those players were good, as good as I saw at Leeds or anywhere else in professional football in England. The one thing many of them did not have was integrity. When they were close to black areas of the stadium, they would mouth abuse at the spectators in those areas. Disgraceful and unacceptable behaviour. The only difference to the everyday attitude and violence on the streets and that surrounding South African football was that it was more organised. If football hooliganism ever organises itself here in England, then it will be very powerful and difficult to overcome.

At the time, Albert was totally unaware that football hooliganism, in England in particular, had increased in its strength of numbers. Football associated literature pertaining to hooliganism has, in the decade since Albert passed away, overwhelmed bookshelves. I have yet to read a volume that truly depicts the reality of how it was. None add anything to the reality of the matter and most are fabricated to suit the writer's own needs and ego. It seems that every club has to have a 'firm' and each associated book proves them to be the toughest of their era. It's all utter nonsense of course, bravado and, in many cases, less than articulate boys bragging.

It goes without saying that in more recent years, the passion both on and off the pitch, has been removed from the game by the respective authorities. Football at its highest level in Britain is nothing but a political tool, used as a vehicle for propaganda and filled with rules and laws that ultimately inhibit the fans' enjoyment of supporting your team, and watching a game that essentially hasn't changed in over a century. It is a very simple game that anyone can play, that has been made extremely complicated.

Now, before we go to a game we have to consider a wealth of inane rules and regulations that, if not maintained, could lead to us being arrested and banned from football watching for life. Ban the terracing, ban the hooligans, ban alcohol, ban smoking, ban singing, ban foul language, ban standing up, ban wearing club colours, ban flags, ban banners, ban cameras, ban bottle tops, ban little ones sitting on the perimeter wall, ban leaping up and down and waving your arms about in celebration. It's ridiculous, and as if that wasn't enough, there is an army of CCTV cameras constantly watching and monitoring our movements.

Whilst I fully appreciate that there exists an unruly element who are determined to cause trouble at football, and security measures are required to 'police' these people, going to football nowadays can be a stressful and uncomfortable experience. Without any doubt there exists in today's game, a 'them and us' situation. They take our money, give us no choices and expect us not to complain if we feel shortchanged by the underachievers representing us on the field of play. We, the supporters, are being systematically suppressed by authoritarian attitudes. If we don't like it, there is nothing we can do, except not go and support our team.

Over the years as a football fan I have witnessed and

suffered the abuse of the authorities, I've seen oppressive policing tactics that are meant to intimidate and ultimately cause an adverse reaction from individual supporters. Most football supporters don't react to such unprofessional methods of control, they have more sense and know what certain police officers' intentions are.

Likewise, the action of stewards is less than acceptable, if they don't like the look of your face then forget it, you will be watched throughout the game, in the vain hope that you commit some serious misdemeanour like dropping a chocolate bar wrapper on the floor, or swearing. Then they pounce, and you are out. It may sound anti-establishment (which I confess I am, certainly when it abuses its authority to the detriment of innocent persons) however, I have witnessed everything from murder through to wrongful and unlawful arrests at football. Speak out against it and you find yourself arrested and in trouble. That's the system authority and political Britain has created for us and to which we have to acquiesce or face a lifetime's exclusion from football.

The vast majority of us don't appreciate the Big Brother state where our every move is monitored and recorded on government databases then used against us when necessary.

Imagine then what it must be like when, for no good reason you are targeted 24 hours a day by society itself: there is no escape, no place to hide, no one to talk to for support. Everywhere you go you are treated as an inferior, called hurtful names, spat upon, excluded, ostracised, a place where your money doesn't buy the same quality or customer service, as that of a fellow human being. Where could this place possibly be? In some far off continent perhaps? Maybe it's a product of an overactive imagination, a place in a novel? Perhaps it doesn't matter where that place is because it's somewhere we believe will never visit.

Think again, the chances are you are already living in that society. That place was the Britain Albert Johanneson arrived in.

I am not a big enough, nor a great enough man to be able to judge the actions or treatment of how one person treats their fellows. The greater majority of people live and lead their lives according to rules and laws, I don't know many who are brave enough, some may say stupid enough, to question why those rules exist, or if they are correct in the way they have been compiled and acted upon.

I am though a human being, I may be black, I may look different, I may speak differently, I may not have had the upbringing of more privileged people, or have the academic qualifications of others, yet I bleed, I laugh, I cry, I love, I know right from wrong, just as every other sensible human being on this earth does. Yet all my life people have, and do, treat me differently. Many treat me and my fellow black Africans with hatred, real animosity. They kick me, spit upon me, beat me, break my skin and my bones, abuse me, call me names, banish me, ostracise me and seemingly believe it is alright to do that.

I can find it within myself to forgive them, but I will I never forget what they have done to me and to thousands of other black Africans like me. My own conscience is clean, theirs can never be.

I cannot recall a single football match that I attended as a young child in South Africa, where violence didn't occur. It wasn't a good environment, women rarely attended organised games, many of my friends believed that we were taken as children, to make us all the more aware of the constant danger that existed around us and to feed the anti-white propaganda that existed. I can always remember Eddie Bryant, he was one of my childhood friends. His father told us he had gone to a game at the Bantu Sports Club in Johannesburg, and when the fans had rioted over various decisions made by the referee, the poor man was murdered right there on the pitch apparently!

There was little or no respect for human life, black or white. Some people carried a 'knobkerrie' to defend themselves, a fighting stick as we called it, it had a rounded knob at one end. This was a very dangerous instrument; it was a weapon. In the townships, gangs of youths would roam the streets, beating others in an attempt to claim superiority of an area. Eventually, some of the tougher gangs introduced fist fighting and boxing onto the streets, thereafter, the violence became all the more physical and personal. It was a tough world and existence.

\* \* \* \* \*

To my utmost surprise, from the many trips I made to South Africa, I was able to track down and speak to many of Albert's childhood friends, many had remained in South Africa, others had moved on to other major cities like Durban and Cape Town. Eddie wasn't the easiest man to locate. With an unhealthy drinking habit, his memory wasn't all it could be. However, his 'pal' Albert was a celebrity and therefore, he had some recollections:

Albert preferred to be called Louis, his father's name, that's how I always knew him. He was a good looking boy, he had, as a child, the look of absolute innocence, almost angel like. No one would suspect he was such a lively character, cheeky really. I remember us helping out by cleaning the floor of a local store, it was on your hands and knees work, scrubbing away to keep the floor clean. Customers would come into the shop and kick us out of their way. Louis got fed up with being treated like this. He said to me, 'I'm going to make a mess of the next person who kicks me out of the way, just you watch.' Within minutes, a well dressed Afrikaan man walks into the shop, instinctively, he kicks out at Louis and moves him aside with his foot, it; was a violent kick. Louis, quick as a flash, had the bucket in his hand and poured it over the man's shoes pretending it to be an accident. The man didn't notice at first, which irritated Louis, so he got the soap, pretended to slip onto the man and plastered the back of the man's trousers in the stuff. Still the man paid no real attention, he looked down and dismissed the apologetic looking Louis with a cold stare.

He could be wild as a young boy. I think more than any of us, he was the one who had a real brain, he had a way about him that made other people listen, not assertive, just clear in what he said and how he acted. People talk about Mandela, Louis had a presence when he was a kid, if he had the resources Mandela had, I firmly believe he could have been a leader. In his own way he was. He wasn't an advocate of violence or confrontation, he would avoid it whenever he could, he would talk others down from fighting mode too.

Then there was that reckless side to him, we would break into cars and steal from them, then sell on what we had stolen. We all did it, we had to, to survive. Louis was inside the car when the owner came out. He jumped into the back seat and hid on the floor. The man got into his car and drove off, with Louis still inside! We were hiding in the dark, worried about our friend. It was perhaps half an hour before the car returned, the man jumped out and went indoors. Moments later, clambering out of the rear window, appears Louis, laughing and full of smiles. He hadn't been seen or found, nor had he taken anything from the car, he said the man made good music and he liked that, he respected that, so he wouldn't take anything from him.

Jim was another friend from that time:

Many people here still refer to Albert as Louis, that was how he was then known to us, he liked being called after his father, but Albert will always be Albert to me. I was a sporty sort of youngster, I loved competition, running, jumping, football, you name it anything competitive and non violent. I worked really hard at it because I saw it as an opportunity to do well and to get out.

As kids we would challenge each other to various games, things like running, or jumping the longest distance or who could throw stones the furthest. Each and every time I went up against Albert, he would beat me. He had this winning mentality when it came to anything sports related. I don't know how mind you, because he never really did a lot to keep himself fit, it just came naturally to him.

In one running race, I expect you would call it a test of stamina since it was over a long distance, he was gone and was out of sight before I had taken my first breath. By the time I reached the finishing point, he would be sat down relaxing and laughing at my late arrival. It was so frustrating competing against him at anything.

The strangest thing of all was how he never used to get involved with the football games we played as kids, it just wasn't him, he said it didn't appeal to his appetite, as it got too congested and he felt suffocated at not being able to run and outperform people who were clearly slower and not as athletic as he was. Yet he went on to become a professional footballer in England with one of their top clubs too. Typical of Albert really.

Alain was another of Albert's friends who was surprised that he became a professional footballer:

Albert was never into physical confrontation, he despised it and I lost count of the number of times he backed out of play fights. He was a wise owl and practised his running almost every day, not that it was planned, you would see him tirelessly pounding the roads and wastelands, it was almost as though he was fleeing or being chased by something. They would have had to be super fast to catch Albert, even on a bad day he could fly, those skinny little legs of his frantically galloping along. It was a sight I could never forget.

He had this notion that his speed and stamina would give him freedom and allow him to achieve his dreams. He was right too, he did, I don't think he, or anyone else who knew him when he was a youngster, expected it to be in football. By all accounts, he was good at that in England, so maybe all that running was the right thing for him, to get to where he wanted to be. He was an achiever and that made him stand out. If he ever lost at anything, he would push himself to improve and practise until he got better.

# 2

# Worlds Apart

The South Africa where Albert Johanneson grew up and was raised is in the main vastly different from the cosmopolitan and bustling country it is today. During my visits there, I found the vast majority of the people welcoming and open about their passion for football and refreshingly, there is a deep rooted pride and loyalty, and wholehearted support for successful exports, be that in business, sport or leisure, commodities or people. It is an environment so unlike Britain, where there is a tendency, particularly in certain parts of the media and society, to undermine negatively anyone or anything that is successful. Here, many enjoy seeing the successful fall from grace, whether it's because they are jealous or envious because they could never achieve. I don't know, but it is common practice to welcome the downfall of one who has positively achieved.

One needs look no further than the demise of my club, Leeds United, during the latter stages of the Peter Ridsdale years, yes we lived the dream, well almost, but when the wheels well and truly came off, almost all of football, players, managers, media and fans alike, revelled in the satisfaction of seeing a club like Leeds collapse.

To this day, there are people out there, possibly reading this book, that still gloat at the club's relegation and ignominious fall through the leagues. If you were a Leeds supporter, it wasn't a good place to be, the suffering and pain we all felt wasn't humorous or remotely funny. It was like sitting on a rollercoaster ride to hell, with bad news followed by more bad news or even worse news. There was only one way we were headed, downwards, and it appeared no one was interested in stopping the freefall. All that came from the boardroom was the apportioning of blame and excuses, as the club changed hands several times, before Ken Bates intervened and stabilised affairs.

During that freefall, some players abandoned the club like rats fleeing a sinking ship, others saw it as an opportunity to reinforce the club's contractual obligations and grab what money there was before disappearing into the sunset to what can only be viewed as lesser clubs. Loyalty to the club or shirt wasn't that obvious to the fans, and players who were once viewed as local heroes, were criticised and became despised. It should be said, the abuse they suffered wasn't acceptable, yet it was nothing when compared to that endured by Albert during his playing days, let alone beyond that time.

South Africa hasn't always been such an open and welcoming place and it has a chequered and somewhat sinister history. As a country it has always had an abundance of natural resources from which its economy depends. Notwithstanding its fertile and established farm lands, there are other resources such as coal, gold and diamond mining and the vast majority of the world's platinum comes from the country. It was originally colonised by the English and the Dutch during the 17th century with the English leading and dominating the country's administration. The Dutch, who were more commonly referred to as Boers or Afrikaners, were forced to establish new colonies and so Orange Free State and Transvaal came into being. In the latter part of the 19th century an abundance of diamonds was discovered in these areas, causing the English to demand access in order to mine the precious stone. The Boers, realising the financial value and economic wealth that prevailed as a result of the diamonds, resisted the

English advances, which was the catalyst for an invasion and so on 11 October 1899 began the Boer War.

Initially the British Army deployed 12,546 men to the hostilities in the region and, by the time the war was officially over on 31 May 1902, there were some 448,435 British troops there. The war itself was anything but straightforward, with the Boers, rather than using contemporary stand and fight techniques, adopting 'hit and run' strategies which seriously damaged the British effort. It is claimed that over 21,000 British troops died as a result of the war, the vast majority of these (13,139) because of the lack of hygiene and proper health care, died of disease. From the Dutch perspective, the statistics are far more depressing with an estimate figure of 53,000 Boers dying as a result of the same confrontation.

In May 1910, the two British colonies, Natal and Cape united with the republics of Transvaal and Orange Free State to create the Union of South Africa which was governed by the British. The black communities were given little or no rights and, other than in Cape, had no say or voting power. They were the silent majority and very much dismissed by the white population.

The first ever prime minister of the Union of South Africa was the Boer leader, General Louis Botha. Botha was anything but fair, his aim was white supremacy in all areas of the country, and he introduced the Masters and Servants Act which saw skilled work for whites only. The Land Act soon followed in 1913, this was an effort to force the black communities away from the business centre districts and thriving city regions, and established 90 per cent of the country for white ownership only.

Understandably, the black people of South Africa protested for equal rights, falsely believing that once the majority of white people understood their plight they would listen and help. Despite the forming of the South

African Native National Congress (SANCC) in 1912 (later to become in 1923 the African National Congress) nothing changed. The government and the white communities continued to demean the black community and ignore the dreadful life conditions they suffered. There was widespread belief that the government wanted to enslave all black South Africans.

Over the years that followed, independence from Britain was established yet the political situation within the country didn't improve with black communities remaining as spectators to the political governance of the country. Two political parties, the National Party led by J.B.M. Hertzhog, and the South African Party, led by Jan Smuts, shared the power under the banner name of the United Party, until the outset of the Second World War when the coalition fell apart and Jan Smuts formed a government.

This was the highly volatile and less than satisfactory political environment that Albert Louis Johanneson was born into. His formative childhood years were filled with the sad divisions caused by apartheid (apartness, separateness) which although it had been in existence for several decades, became formally recognised on 4 June 1948, when the Afrikaner Nationalist Party of South Africa came into power. Led by Daniel Francoise Malan, the party formally introduced various policies and acts which cemented apartheid into the foundations of everyday life in the country.

Initially there was the Prohibition of Mixed Marriages Act, 1949, and Immorality Act, 1950, these were government initiatives towards institutionalising racial differentiation into society.

Fundamentally, the acts dictated the prohibition of sexual intercourse and marriage between whites and blacks. Then there was the introduction of identity cards, a scheme where all people over the age of sixteen were required to carry with them at all times, a formal identity card that contained their personal details. The content effectively organised them into groups of various racial categories.

The Groups Areas Act of 1950 prohibited and restricted the entrance of blacks into the urban, industrial, and agricultural areas, which were declared all white areas and actively policed to ensure that no unlawful access could be gained. To be in such areas the pass holder had to have state permission, essentially, those that had such authority and permission were black people who carried out menial roles for white households.

The Population Registration Act, 1950, dictated that all Africans were classified into three categories, each according to their race: Bantu (black), Coloured (mixed race), or White. The government carried out the assessments and so classified individuals on the basis of such things as education, appearance, habits and manner. Once categorised, rules were dictated according to the individual race and these had to be strictly adhered to. Anyone found breaking such laws potentially faced death through to punishments that ranged from, whipping, stoning, and beating, to imprisonment.

The Abolition of Passes and Coordination of Documents Act, 1952, required all Africans to carry a pass book, similar to a passport (Dompas). The pass book was another item that contained all of the holder's personal information: name, photograph, height, fingerprints. It also provided a detailed explanation on the individual's employment rights, and where they had been employed, and their performance at work. If black South Africans failed to obey the rules, they were removed from the area, and their crime reported in the pass book. The penalty for not carrying the pass book at all times was equally as severe, and ranged from imprisonment and monetary fines, to a torturous death.

Everything was heavily weighted against the black population and one can only imagine how difficult everyday life must have been for those suffering such abuse.

> I cannot say that I was, or am politically minded, although I do know what is right and what is wrong. The way black people were treated in South Africa during the time of my childhood was wrong, and like many others I did express my opinion and make a stand against the oppression.
>
> As I grew up, I found life becoming increasingly more unbearable on the streets of the Johannesburg district; far too many people were disappearing, murdered as a result of the oppressive politics of the country. We had very little to laugh or feel comfortable about, we had no future and weren't allowed to have any ambition. Yet we did laugh, we did make the most of our lives, and we did many different things that made our lives more bearable.
>
> My main focus as I grew up was to get money for the family. To be honest, I wasn't too bothered how I acquired or got it or how I made it, as long as I could contribute positively to the welfare of the household I felt as though I was doing my part and achieving something. It's important to achieve something each day in your life, no matter how small or insignificant it may seem, it is something that you have done and when you reflect back upon your day, it is very likely that it will give you a feeling of satisfaction and make you feel better.
>
> One of the first things I taught myself, was how to get into cars and efficiently strip parts from them, these could either be sold for money or anonymously given to my father. I knew that procurement of car parts greatly helped him in his work, since it meant he didn't have to pay any money out in advance to purchase the required components. I would listen carefully to him as he worked on the motors, he would explain what each part did and its relevance and importance to the effective running of

the car. Mentally, I noted everything he said and would quickly identify the bits needed and without him knowing, go out and get them. He pretended he had no idea I was doing it, but deep down, he must have known.

One of the most difficult parts of this scheme was leaving the acquired parts in a place where he could find them without him physically catching me with them in my possession. More than once, I got a part, only to find it was for the wrong model or he had already fitted a replacement. It wasn't as if I could simply go out and return them from whence they came!

I was astute as a kid, shrewd, you had to be to survive. The thing was, I knew a secret way to access the white areas without ever being seen, and it helped that I could run of course. It was a matter of crossing through the rear yards of white people's property at night. I knew from different journeys into that territory where all the different kind of motors were, I knew the streets and yard locations like the back of my hand. I even knew where the noisy dogs were kept so tried to avoid them since their incessant barking could alert a house owner that something was wrong. It really wasn't worth taking the risk of trying to deceive such dogs, best to avoid at all costs.

There were many tales and stories about kids who got caught raiding white people areas, some suffered a beating, others just disappeared! Presumably killed and their bodies dumped somewhere for scavenging animals to consume. Whatever, I didn't ever want to find myself in a situation where I could confirm or deny any such tale. Getting caught wasn't on my agenda.

Occasionally I would be disturbed during a raid and I would have to hide before running away when the coast was clear. There was one time when I stole into the white man's land in search of a specific type of radiator hose (top and bottom). I soon found the right model of car and quietly crawled beneath its engine compartment and began to loosen off the hose. As I pulled it away from the radiator, the engine coolant water poured out. It was piping hot, the car engine hadn't yet cooled down and I burned my hand and my neck as both took the brunt of the hurt. I yelped in pain.

Within seconds, I heard people coming out of their homes to see what the commotion was. It was too late to flee, my only option was to hide. To secrete myself from sight completely, I crawled further under the engine bay, keeping my feet well hidden and lodged inside a wheel. My heart was pounding and I was certain that I was about to be caught. It was one of the scariest moments I ever had because the inquisitive neighbours came directly to the car beneath which I lay. I could see the feet and legs of at least half a dozen people who had gathered around the front of the car. My clothes had been saturated by the water that had come out of the radiator and thankfully none of those gathered noticed the surplus radiator water running out from beneath the car. I was terrified to move or breathe.

I heard one of the group say, 'If it's a 'darkie' then we should kill the bastard slowly and dump his body back inside the township, make an example of him to the others.' You can imagine how frightened I was on hearing this. I was still a child, maybe only ten or eleven!

After a few minutes of chatting, they returned to their homes, again I was alone in the darkness. I lay there for quite a while until I sensed it was okay to resume what I had come to achieve. With great haste I stripped the entire radiator from the car, as it was easier to do this than try to disconnect the top hose. Extricating myself from beneath the motor, I slipped it into a sack and waited. White people would think nothing of using a gun on a black person in their area at night, so it was an important aspect of survival to make sure there was an escape route readily available and clear.

With the radiator wrapped in a sack, I ran all the way home, leaping fences across the rear yards of ten or fifteen white men's properties. There I placed the radiator beside the car being repaired, for my father to find the following day. It was wonderful and made me feel very happy to see his face light up with joy when he found the part. As always, he prayed to thank the Lord for delivering such gracious giving.

It wasn't all doom, gloom and despondency, I recall the marriage of a girl named Sumu, who was in a relationship with a man called Dan. His actual name wasn't Dan at all, that was his adopted identity. People would do that to gain a reputation associated with the name, and also for the sake of recognition. Dan and Sumu were married and the unison was celebrated by hundreds of people in the streets. It was like a carnival.

That wedding was the first time I ever danced to music, and I loved it. The sound and beat of the music was incredible, I found my feet tapping and my body rhythmically gliding as I danced in the street for hours. Everywhere I looked there was a willing female partner waiting for their turn to dance with me. One woman, Ida, was a teacher at the school I intermittently attended. Ida told me that I had rhythm that came from my soul and I was a natural dancer. I was thrilled to hear something so positive. Ida taught me how to dance properly, how to hold a female partner and how to glide across the ground, all this was achieved on the dirt track roads of the township. It was anything but a modern wooden ballroom.

Much of the music came over the crackly airwaves of radio; a lot from the occasional gramophone player that some families were fortunate enough to have acquired. Every so often, I would hear the music drifting out of homes and out across the night sky of the townships. It seemed to arouse a sense of calm everywhere. It caused people to smile or reflect because music can play an important role in the lives of most people.

I didn't consider myself to be a good dancer and it was more likely that Ida was telling me I was because she thought she had found herself a dance partner! I danced because I enjoyed it, it allowed me a small amount of freedom of expression. I wasn't bothered if people laughed at my dancing or movement to the beat, it pleased me, and that was all that mattered. My favoured music of that time, as I remember, was the songs played by artistes such as: Jimmy Dorsey, Vaughn Monroe, Harry James, Duke Ellington, Billie Holiday, and the great Glenn Miller. There was even some Bing Crosby in there. To this day I listen to those same tunes and it takes me right back there. Dancing is one of the greatest things anybody can achieve; it is like physical poetry, gliding and moving gracefully is a real skill.

The public and political unrest in the country hit a new low when in 1956, the South African police arrested some 156 political leaders, these included established campaigners, Luthuli, Mandela, Tambo, Sisulu, and many others. The government placed the political prisoners on trial for treason which consisted of 23 different acts of sabotage and conspiring to overthrow the government. It was alleged that the group had in their possession or control, 48,000 Soviet made anti-personnel mines, and 210,000 hand grenades! A protracted court case that was to drag on for five years followed. Mandela in particular was a person the government wanted to silence. He had joined the African National Congress in 1942 and had persuaded them to focus on boycotts and strikes to get the powers-that-be to take notice. With a passionate desire to help the entire black community of South Africa, Mandela achieved what he could to combat apartheid. He also trained as a lawyer so that he could understand and properly use the law to undermine, and bring into question the legality of what was happening to black South Africans in the country.

On the 21st of March 1960, one of the worst public atrocities to occur in South African history took place during a peaceful protest against the pass laws in Sharpeville. An initial group of approximately 7,000 black people congregated. They refused to carry their 'dompas' and offered themselves up for arrest. It was said that it was a peaceful demonstration to show the authorities the quantity of black people who opposed the said law. The police and the authorities claimed otherwise, stating that telephone lines into Sharpeville were cut and as the crowd swelled in numbers to approximately 20,000 the situation became distressing and volatile. Bricks and stones were thrown at the vastly outnumbered armed police officers, who had swelled their numbers to approximately 130 by calling in reinforcements.

One junior officer, no doubt recalling the murder of nine police officers at Cato Manor, panicked and fearing for his safety, fired off a volley of shots into crowd. This caused other police officers to fire, and dozens randomly shot into the gathered demonstrators who were now fleeing for their lives. It was utter carnage. In a 40-second barrage of bullets, 69 black people were killed, including 10 children. A further 19 children were injured. A high majority of people killed and wounded were shot in the back, trying to escape the scene! The police commanding officer at the scene, Lieutenant Colonel Pienaar, later denied giving the order to fire and dismissed the rumour that it was a peaceful demonstration with a damning statement. 'The native mentality does not allow them to gather for a peaceful demonstration. For them to gather means violence.'

There was political and public outrage at the news of the massacre. The white ruling government immediately banned the African National Congress from all such activity, forcing people like Nelson Mandela underground to continue the fight. He went on to create Umkhonto we Sizwe (which translated means: Spear of the Nation, it is also more commonly abbreviated into MK). This was a military aspect of the African National Congress, and Mandela organised disciplined military training in nearby Algeria for each of its members. It was during a return trip from Algeria that he was arrested for going between countries without a passport and he was later tried for sabotage and trying to overthrow the government.

I am not a big enough or a great enough man to be able to judge the actions or treatment of how one person treats their fellows. The greater majority of people live and lead their lives according to rules and laws. I don't know many who are brave enough, some may say stupid enough, to question why those rules exist, or even if they are right in the way that they have been compiled and policed. I am a human being, I may be black, I may look different, I may speak differently, I may not have had the upbringing of more privileged people, or hold the academic qualifications of others who see that as a standard, yet I bleed, I laugh, I cry, I love. I know right from wrong just as every other human being on this earth must. Yet throughout my life people have treated me differently, many treat me and my fellow black Africans with hatred and animosity. They kick me, spit upon me, beat me, break my skin and my bones, abuse me, call me names, banish me, ostracise me. I can find it within myself to forgive them, but I will never forget what they have done to me and to thousands of other black Africans like me. My conscience is clean, theirs can never be.

I was shocked by the level one human being will stoop to obtain control over one of their fellows, the official and formal history of South Africa is well documented and the brief overview of that history, contained in this volume is not meant to create new fact or detail, it is simply to illustrate how terrifying life in South Africa was and how everyday life for black people had deteriorated so badly.

I began to rationalise the world I lived in as I grew older. By the time I was a teenager I understood that South Africa was one very biased and politically corrupt country. I understood the complexities of politics but could never appreciate why or how black people suffered so much more than their white counterparts. I wanted what every black person in South Africa yearned for, equality.

Like many others of my era, I followed the word of Nelson Mandela, he is a great leader and a man who is both driven and determined. I was at a campaign gathering in the 1950s and saw the state move in and arrest him. Collectively as a group, we found ourselves surrounded by gun toting police who needed no encouragement to shoot. I remained very still and had my hands in the air. I wouldn't make eye contact with the police, since I knew how sensitive they could be to being looked at by black people. I knew that to do so could escalate matters and cause another massacre.

Mandela and others were taken away, and once they had gone, the police moved out and left us to our own devices. However, without any leader or public speaker to arouse and rally us, we drifted away to our own homes. To this day I still revere Nelson Mandela. He will always be something very special to me because he fought for our cause.

I knew people who went to Sharpeville for the demonstration. What the government came out and said afterwards was so wrong. The people I knew were not hooligans or rioters, they were family people who wanted a bright future for their children, and not a depressing, repressed state where there was no options and, who the government didn't care about in an out of sight, out of mind kind of way. I was told by people who were there that it was the authorities who were at fault. They couldn't handle or disperse the crowd and so resorted to what they knew best, brutality and murder.

I know that is a strong and powerful statement or assertion to make, yet it is true. What else can you call the killing of innocent men, women and children who had no weapons and had no desire to cause harm? They simply wanted to be heard and the government to acknowledge their voice. The authorities sprayed bullets at people who were running away from them, knowing that there would be fatalities, they were reckless and it was inhumane slaughter, and for what purpose, control and power!

One of the things that helped me temporarily forget the death and heartache that surrounded us each day was benzine. I'm ashamed to mention it really, yet it was something that we all did. Benzine was a bit like petrol or should I say methylated spirits, it was easy to get hold of across South Africa. We would pour it into jars or containers, prick holes in the top and cover our heads with jumpers or shirts so as to concentrate the vapours and help us inhale or sniff it in. It made us very happy and carefree, until it began to wear off, then there were headaches and tearful eyes.

I don't ascribe to anyone doing things like that, but you have to understand back then in South Africa we had very little else to occupy ourselves with. It was a good high when you were there, but very bad when you come back down. I remember the constant feeling of giddiness, sickness and nausea, not very nice really, but it did give you a lift for a short time.

Once we were sat in a group sniffing the stuff when an adult wandered over, we thought we were going to get a telling off. He asked what we were up to and so we explained we were taking in benzine. He laughed and asked us if he minded if he joined us? It wasn't a problem for us at all and so he enjoyed a session with us. It was something that was kind of acceptable then, and to be perfectly honest, there were some days when you would see people laying all over the place, laughing and smiling contently to themselves, as high as kites on the stuff.

Whenever I went out with my brother Trevor he would enjoy the benzine too, not that it matters, but he probably enjoyed it a bit more than I did. He is a real character is Trevor and we got into loads of bother as kids do, but when the chips were down, as all families should, we devoutly defended and protected one another.

As I grew up, the need for benzine grew less and less. I enjoyed having the occasional smoke and sneaking the odd beer whenever one was available, it was only recreational and bit of fun, a learning process that we all went through. I actually stopped smoking when I first arrived at Leeds, though I did later succumb to the nicotine habit. Then one day I witnessed something that put everything in my life into perspective. A police car was chasing a sprinting black youth, the kid was all over the place, his legs were unstable and were wobbling beneath him like rubber bands. I don't know how long the chase had been going on for, but he looked exhausted. Then he suddenly stopped running, he catapulted forward and dropped to the floor like a dead weight. I wanted to go over to help, but the police car was there and so I thought it best to leave well alone.

One of the policemen called me over and asked me if I knew who the youth was, when I got to him I saw the boy laid there, his face had a blue tint to it and it was swollen. His eyes were massive, staring and almost popping out of his head, they were bloodshot, and he was cut to ribbons from the fall I had seen him make. I took a gulp as I did know the youth, I knew him as 'Nervous Norman' He was so called because he was just that, nervous. Always twitching and jumping from one foot to the other. He was a bit of a strange youth, quiet and withdrawn, the one thing I knew he wasn't was violent or confrontational.

The policeman again asked me if I knew who he was. I was taken aback because he was referring to 'Nervous Norman' in the past tense. I asked if he was okay to which one of the policemen stood up, roughly kicked his head and told me he was 'very dead.' I felt sick and vomited on the road. The other policeman was okay, he showed a bit of concern about me, and I told him that I knew who the youth was. I asked why he was that funny colour and what had he been doing for them to chase him. It transpired that, 'Nervous Norman' had been playing with little kids, four or five-year-olds and had been caught giving them benzine. The police were unsure what his motive was for doing this but when they approached him to make an arrest, he up and legged it until he dropped dead in mid-flight so to speak!

It was a lot to take in, seeing someone who was the same age as me, drop dead like that shocked me and the way Norman's face looked is something I can never forget. It was blue and all puffed up as though someone had stuck a pump into his mouth and inflated him with air. I was told this was caused by the effect of the drugs in his body and the lack of oxygen as he ran and ran in an attempt to escape capture. Poor Norman, his body lay there for several hours before it was picked up. It later turned out that his family had kicked him out and abandoned him. He was living on his own in a shack which consisted of a series of wooden doors nailed together to form a hut shape. I never touched benzine again after that.

I told myself that I never wanted to end up like Norman and instead of doing daft things like the benzine or smoking too much, I took to running and getting myself in shape. I wanted a happy balance in my life and so opted to try to find some work. The best I could do was fixing shoes or helping mend cars, neither job paid particularly well, in fact when it was my father who I was helping, it didn't pay at all. It was 'character building' he would tell me.

My interests changed as I grew older, and soon I was becoming friendly with girls and developing new relationships, the usual sort of stuff you do as you get to your early teens. It was a pleasant distraction from everyday life, and I would sit and tell my dreams and aspirations to some of those who I walked out with. I had my favourites but would never divulge who or what we discussed. That was personal stuff between us, it's not for a book.

I sensed Albert was beginning to find some enjoyment in recounting some of his teenage life, certainly, when he recalled some tales, he had a certain sparkle in his eye, and on more than one occasion I became aware of him puffing out his chest with pride. It was great to know that deep inside the man I was talking to, lay the real Albert Johanneson, the man for whom I searched.

Many of my childhood friends moved away or simply went missing, and as my own interests changed so did my friendships. I began to hang about with people who were more focused on sport and had a winning way about them. We would race in groups, sometimes it was for a few blocks, on others it was for several miles.

I don't remember ever coming last in those races, especially not the long distance ones, I always won those. Chez was one of the better runners in our group, he told me that I could go even faster if I learned how to use my feet better. His father was a runner too, and he showed us some training he had created for his feet. This was to make them more articulate and dexterous. I watched and learned.

Eventually I found myself trying new ways to develop my feet coordination. I had a box full of old tennis style balls, I would stand in front of a wall and kick the tiny ball at it, eventually developing different techniques such as taking the pace out of the rebounding ball, flicking it up in the air and then balancing it on top of my foot. Later I could flick it up onto my head and balance it on my forehead without ever using my hands. Me and those balls, I loved them and I must have spent four or five hours a day practising.

I was a bit shocked when one day, one of the boys from a different group came over to me and told me I was the best footballer he had ever seen. Football, I thought, football, I don't even like the sport, it's for white men and I'm no footballer. I thanked him for the compliment, even if it wasn't one I accepted it for what it was. He asked if I could help train him to do some of the things I practised because he desperately wanted to become a footballer. For days I tried to teach him, but he never seemed to have any control over the ball. I explained to him that initially it was eye and feet coordination that was important, the dexterity of the feet would come once he had mastered that. He didn't really appreciate that advice, he just thought he could do the tricks without putting any work into it.

When it got dark I would use the lights from shop windows to illuminate a training area. I had learned that it was more difficult a skill at night when the light was disappearing and the ball wasn't so obvious. It was great fun and all the time I knew it was helping me to develop my own skills and coordination.

After a time, I used to get a regular crowd of people who would come to watch me practise. They would clap some of the more difficult tricks I completed and that really inspired me to push on. Getting rewarded with a round of applause for doing something I enjoyed was a good feeling, I wanted to please them all the more and so continued to train with the ball. I began to run with it at my feet, it sounds simple enough but don't forget it was a tennis ball I was using, and the ground in the places where I was training wasn't exactly flat. It was rugged and bumpy, stones and rocks protruded from the hard surface; there was no grass as such.

Eventually I got the hang of it and was soon keeping the ball under control and lifting over the bumps and lumps with my feet and doing my little flicks at the same time. The ball and I were as one and I would challenge people to try to take it from me. They couldn't, as I would twist and turn and spin round then sprint off, the ball still at my feet. I became a bit of a local act and people came from all over Germiston and bet money on whether I would achieve more difficult tasks with the ball. Not that I saw any money, it was always others who did the gambling. I was tasked with more and more new challenges and with these came time limitations to achieve them. The crowd, only a handful of people, would shout at me 'Hurry, hurry.' That stuck with me because I was later referred to in Germiston as, Albert 'Hurry-Hurry' Johanneson.

It all became a bit boring after a while, there is only so much you can do with a tennis ball and local people didn't really find it riveting entertainment. I began to train elsewhere, throwing the ball high in the sky and trapping it dead as it hit the ground or killing its pace with my foot and keeping it under control. It was during one such session that a man approached me and asked me if I wanted a game of football. He was from a team known as Shamrocks, the team was short of one player and they desperately needed someone to fill in. I explained that I had no boots and would have to play barefoot. He wasn't bothered by this and told me to follow him. It was such a long time since I had played in a football match, and the last time hadn't been a great experience for me. I was marked out of the game by a beast of a full back who kicked me ten feet in the air every time I went near him. In the end, through frustration, I gave up trying to play football against him. It was all he could do, kick me!

I was surprised to see that the game I was to appear in hadn't yet started, they were waiting for me. I pulled on the jersey and was soon lining up on the pitch. The rest of the players seemed much older and bigger than I was and recollections of being kicked came flooding back to me. Early on in the game I got the ball passed to me, it looked massive compared to the tennis ball I was used to. As I controlled the ball, I looked up and saw a huge gap open up behind an oncoming opposition player. I waited for him to commit to the challenge before flicking the ball past him and pushing it ahead of me down the wing. Another challenge came in from the right, but before he could clatter into me, I had stopped in my tracks, causing him to go flying in front of me and calling me a bastard in his frustration.

I looked up towards the penalty area and saw our centre forward, a man called Cliff, rushing towards the goal. I chipped the ball forward, directly onto his head, and he nodded it into the goal. We had scored and I became an instant success. I was loving it, there was freedom and space to exploit and as the game progressed I found myself growing in confidence and self belief.

Our opponents were a tough and resilient lot and equalised before half time. It was an immediate change of ends at half time, no real break of sorts, and we were soon back playing. It looked like it was going to end in a draw as the game became much more strategic and tense. The referee, a friend of one of the players, told us there was two minutes remaining. As the time ticked away, I collected the ball on the halfway line and decided to run at the opposition. I'm not certain how I did it or how it happened, but it all just seemed to open up for me. I was skipping past players and suddenly I was in on goal. The goalkeeper had rushed out from his line to narrow the angle I had available to shoot at; he looked huge stood there before me. I could barely see the frame of the goal behind him, but opted to try to bend it in the one area I could see, the top left corner. I tried to bend my foot around the ball as I struck it firmly. It worked, the ball seemed to curve round beyond the goalkeeper's outstretched arm and hand and dropped into the goal behind him. My team went wild with excitement, and I was mobbed by them and chaired off the pitch as an acknowledgement for my performance.

I was thrilled to have done so well, especially as I had played in my bare feet and many of the other players were all booted up. I could have gone on and played another game, but everyone else seemed satisfied with the game and so went home. I was invited to play the following night when we were taking on a different local side. It was all very informal and there was no pressure, just clean fun.

The games were regular and came thick and fast, and I couldn't get enough of them. Football was allowing me to fulfil my aspiration to do well. After one game, a man who had watched regularly from the sideline approached me. He asked me if I wanted to have a game with a more organised club. He asked me to play for Germiston

Coloured Schools. I agreed and became a regular in that team.

Suddenly, my life took on a whole new meaning, football was providing me a chance to do well. It was while playing for the Coloured School that I was invited to represent the coloured national team in the Kajee Cup Final. A white British coach called 'Topper' Brown was the manager, he had not an ounce of malice nor was he culturally biased in any way. He loved football and wanted us to enjoy it too, he would tell us to play it naturally, let the ball do the work. It was said that 'Topper' had been a professional with Arsenal in England.

Curiously, research indicates that there was no one of that name (Topper Brown) who played for Arsenal or had ever been on the Arsenal books during the era in question. The provenance of his credentials remain doubtful, though his achievement in the South African game are seemingly well documented especially as he did achieve success and was well respected by the black footballers he worked with, most of whom remember him with some affection.

It was a great time for me, I was young enough to have the stamina and fit enough to run around for hours at a time. I won the cup (Kajee) twice, once in 1956 and again in 1960, I was captain and it was a real honour and achievement. Things got better as Germiston Caledonian Society Amateur Football Club invited me to sign for them.

The Callies, are they were better known, were one of the better football sides and clubs, originally founded by Scottish immigrants (who had migrated to South Africa for work which was mainly on the railways or as miners) in 1906. Primarily an all white club, they turned professional in 1959, a matter that had no effect on Albert's career or life.

Although they played in an all white league, black football was becoming more established and some games featuring black footballers did take place. I also represented and captained a team called Hume Zebras who were from Germiston. It wasn't very well organised but at least it offered some more competitive games for me to play in.

I played in the same football side as the cricketer, Basil D'Oliveira. He was a wonderful all-round sportsman, good at everything. He migrated to England in 1960 and went on to be a world class cricketer. I followed him, as a footballer, a year later. Initially, although we moved in different sporting and social circles, we often bumped into each other, and talked of the horrors of apartheid and the anti-black movement in Britain. He didn't seem to suffer the same degree of abuse that I received. Maybe, because cricket audiences are a little more guarded in their vocal support, or maybe because football was more exciting to watch, affordable and appealing to the working class. I'm not sure, but Basil was a man who gained recognition and respect for his cricketing ability. He did much to publicise the wrongs of apartheid in South Africa and promote equality throughout the country. He is someone I and most South African people respect.

I spoke briefly with the legendary cricketer in 1996 and asked him about his recollections of Albert:

I remember Albert Johanneson, he was a wonderfully gifted footballer, possibly the best black footballer to come out of South Africa. Many people speak of me as being pivotal to showing the skill and prowess of black South African sports people, even though I was officially classed in that country as a coloured. It was Albert Johanneson who was the unsung hero of that era, that man has the right to stand proud at the top of the list of black sportsmen who are termed 'ambassadors' for our country. I am proud to say I played alongside him in football games, it was a real privilege and even at that young age, he possessed quality rarely seen in football today.

Quite a reference from such a revered source, Albert would have been proud to be so recognised by someone he often recalled with great fondness and respect. Unfortunately, Basil D'Oliveira passed away on 19 November, 2011.

\* \* \* \* \*

Football in South Africa has a rather chequered history that was consistently based on apartheid and racial difference. Records indicate that in 1862 the first documented football matches were played in Cape Town and Port Elizabeth. These were between white civil servants and soldiers on tour of duty there. The first recognised football club was formed as early as 1879, with the lengthy title of Pietermaritzburg County. The County team was made up solely from the European immigrant population and played friendly fixtures against the various sections of the occupying British troops. They were one of four teams competing in the Natal Football Association that was formed in 1882, with a league comprising of just four clubs – Pietermaritzburg County, Natal Wasps, Durban Alpha and Umgeni Stars.

Elsewhere in the country, the South African Football Association (SAFA), later to be known as the FA of South Africa, was formed in the same year, 1882. In Johannesburg, the Transvaal Football Association was created in 1889, by Dutch immigrants and the principal competition here was the innovatively sounding Transvaal Challenge Cup. Early winners of the competition were; Wanderers Wasps in 1889, Rangers in 1890, 1892, 1893, 1894 and in 1896.

With various independent associations cropping up across the country, there was no amalgamation or integration of competitive leagues. Each association catered for a specific culture, thus the game itself was fragmented and without any formative or overarching administration body. Records, particularly of the 'non-white' leagues and associations are scant and rarely exist, meaning that much history from the black game cannot ever be accurately recorded.

It was to be twenty years later, in 1902 that the South African Indian Football Association (SAIFA) was founded in Kimberley, and a national competition solely for the Indian population, the Sam China Cup, was held.

Another Association, the Johannesburg Bantu Football Association was formed in 1929, followed, in 1932, by the creation of the South African African Football Association (SAAFA) and the inaugural national Bakers Cup competition (in 1937 this was renamed the Moroka-Baloyi Cup). Administrational matters were further complicated during 1933, when a further two, new associations, were formed: The South African Bantu Football Association (SABFA) and the South African Coloured Football Association (SACFA). In a rather futile attempt to coordinate non-white football, in 1935 the Transvaal Inter Race Soccer Board was formed and organised the first representative games between Africans, Indians, and 'Coloureds'. In addition they introduced a competition known as the Suzman Cup.

By 1951 several strategic elements of the non-white game saw fit to join forces as the: SAAFA, SACFA, and South African Indian Football Association SAIFA, came together to form the anti-apartheid focused South African Soccer Federation (SASF). The world's governing football body FIFA under the leadership of Jules Rimet, struck a severe blow to the inter-racial game in South Africa when in 1952, it admitted the all white South African Football Association as one of its members. The message from the football powerhouse that is FIFA was clear and damaging; the game in South Africa was not for non-white players! The membership to FIFA was suspended in 1961 because of its continued segregation policies and refusal to budge from these.

The SASF, relentlessly campaigned and continued to voice its opinion that football should be an all embracing game for all people, and after representation to the International Olympic Committee in Paris in 1955, they received some validation from the committee, with an acknowledgement that discrimination against 'non-white' sports people in South Africa existed. Incredibly, to counter this, in 1956 the South African government introduced its own apartheid sport policy.

In 1959, FASA formed the first South African all white professional league, the National Football League (NFL). It attracted white footballers from overseas, many of who were retiring professionals from the British game. Shamefully, so much prejudice existed that some clubs competing in the NFL, blacks, as well as not being allowed to participate, were also prevented from being spectators!

On the world stage, in 1966, South Africa was included in the draw for the qualifying stages of the World Cup competition, however, being unable and unwilling to field a mixed race side they failed to pursue active involvement. The outcome of this sporting apartheid system, saw South Africa expelled from FIFA and forced to address processes that would see gradual football and sporting integration.

It was no wonder that Albert Johanneson and so many other black South African footballers found it difficult to aspire to, or concentrate on a career in football. Had it not been for the passion and vision of other people in the country, he may never have had any sporting option made available to him.

I didn't know it at the time, but a school teacher and football scout from Benoni, a man called Barney Gaffney, had been following my career, he had first spotted me playing for the Germiston coloured school and later training on my own. Every so often he would appear when I was playing, mostly kicking about really, with other youths in recreational games.

After one game, he approached me and said he could help me refine my game and give me the opportunity to become a professional footballer, possibly in England. It was something I had never considered, playing in England, nor being professional, and now, it did appeal to me, and I was extremely grateful that he should be so interested. I knew of two black players whose names were always mentioned with some reverence during that time, as they had left South Africa to play in Europe: Steve Mokone had gone to Coventry in England, and David Julius went to Sporting Lisbon in Portugal.

I had also seen and witnessed English football first hand, including the legendary Stanley Matthews, when England played South Africa at the Rand in June 1956. Again it was an all white fixture, but it was a huge event for everyone in the country. It was heavily policed in case of any political or black uprising.

In the week leading up to the game there were many reports of outbursts of violence as the authorities told the police to swamp the townships and quieten any political unrest or other local tensions. They achieved this by using force to batter silence into anyone who dared voice an opinion or look likely to think for themselves. Whether the English football authorities would have agreed to play such fixtures knowing that such violence and oppression were taking place because of it, I don't know. I would seriously have hoped not.

Mr Matthews was a great ambassador for England and football, he was very gracious and kind to everyone he met, he did not differentiate between black and white. He said that to him football was a game for people everywhere and everyone should have a right to play and compete in it. That statement earned him a great deal of respect across our nation.

In the 1970s many white British and European players

came over to play for clubs in white South African leagues. It was mainly for the money and the fame they could acquire and not for any kudos South African football offered. The black communities had little or no respect for many of these players, as they were effectively supporting apartheid and perpetuating the divide and ill-feeling between black and white people through football.

Some of my colleagues from Leeds came over here to play after their professional careers in England had finished, it was sometimes referred to as a 'pay day to top up the pension.' Durban was always a big football city, there was a United and a City and a Celtic I think. Durban City was one of the bigger clubs who paid decent money to get players from Europe to play. Morally it was wrong, and it still hurts that people will sell their soul to the devil for the sake of a few pounds. I would always question the moral sensitivity of white European players who joined all white football teams in South Africa. Some pretended to be ignorant of apartheid, others simply didn't care, money was their one focus.

I do have very strong views on this subject and I am correct for having these. If those people had witnessed the oppression and suffering we blacks suffered each day, right up to more recent times, then perhaps they would think differently about taking the money and think more about humanity. Being a black man in those times was hell! Dogs were put on us for merely walking in the suburbs. We were beaten by white people for entertainment . . . they called it 'Kaffir bashing.' Kaffir is still a word I find most insulting, it's the South African equivalent of Nigger, very bad words.

Johnny Haynes was a white British footballer who made a name for himself in South Africa. He played in the all white leagues and was very successful. He was a nice man, personable and knowledgeable about football. I was fortunate to meet him in the 1970s, and we discussed South African football. Sadly, he made a clear distinction of class between black and white footballers. It wasn't what I would call racism and it certainly wasn't meant to offend, yet the inference was that white footballers were better and had more physical resources than black footballers.

I was shocked by this statement and told him that he was wrong, that black football in South Africa was under-resourced by the white governing authorities, therefore the black players had to be stronger, fitter and more skilful to get noticed outside the country. I took a pin and pricked my thumb, causing it to bleed. I held it up to Johnny's face and pointed out that my blood was red in colour like his, I pointed to my legs and told him I had two, as he had. He was clearly surprised by my reaction, and I apologised in case I had caused an offence. He shook my hand and told me I was absolutely right and said he was the one who should apologise as he had worded his comment wrongly. It takes a big man to do that, and I gladly shook his hand and welcomed his apology and understanding.

Other white European players were not so welcoming of such opinion, and I was often told to 'piss off' followed by the derogatory term, 'Nigger' or 'Rastus.' I don't deny that it hurt when I was called names such as that, especially when they were coming from members of my own profession, but after a time, you get to realise that names only hurt if you allow them to and only if you really care what the other person, the name caller, feels or thinks.

I could specifically name two established white England international footballers of the era playing for London-based clubs, who held such disregard for their fellow human beings and were without doubt racist in their views and thoughts towards black footballers. I don't think it was deliberate racism, it had been indoctrinated in them through society and politicians, that black people were different to them in every way. To know that such people felt so strongly about the difference skin colour can make to a person's opinion, truly saddens me, especially when they were held in such high regard by the world of football!

Getting back to Barney Gaffney, some of the lads I played with had heard of, and knew him to be one of the most respected black scouts in the region. So it was great for me that he thought I could make it. He told me from the outset that he alone couldn't turn me into a professional footballer, I had to want it, I had to have desire, passion and commitment, discipline and composure, thereafter the skill element was important too.

It sounded daunting and I wasn't sure I was good enough, yet I realised this was a chance to make something of myself for me and my family.

Barney and I worked on all aspects of my game, he firmly believed that working with a tennis ball was the best kind of workout I could have. He would forcibly throw it at me and get me to take the pace out of the throw and control it. Another of his favourites was to randomly throw it any direction and get me to chase after it and bring it under control within two bounces. It was hard work and he really pushed me to my limits and beyond them at times. For the first time in my life I was physically sick with exhaustion from all the running and exercise. My legs would ache after each session, yet I could see that they were growing stronger and the muscles expanding further as each week went by. He was a fine man and I really respected him for giving me his time and constantly pushing me.

Barney tried to get me to change all aspects of my life, smoking, drinking and the food I would eat. I wasn't going to have that though, I enjoyed a smoke and liked my food. We couldn't really afford to pick and choose my diet. I had what the family had, and that was the end of the matter.

It was around September 1960, when Barney told me that he had been told that scouts from Newcastle United had been to Johannesburg and that I was on their list of players to watch while they were in the city. This meant absolutely nothing to me, so I dismissed it from my thoughts until one day I saw two Englishmen watching a game, they were dressed in suits and ties so stood out from what we were used to seeing.

At half time I was told they were scouts from Newcastle United and they were looking at a lad from the opposition, called 'Nifty Norman.' He was a tall skinny individual who had little or no skill on the ball but had legs that when outstretched I swear, could reach from one side of the goal to the other!

At the end of the game one of the men came up to me and asked who I was. I told him. He asked if I had heard of Newcastle United, I told him that I hadn't and he looked surprised. He told me that he liked the way I played football and he would be in touch with me in a few weeks, as he wanted to see more of what I could do before making a decision on anything. He advised me not to think about either of them watching from the sidelines, just to get on with my usual game. I never saw the men or heard from them again.

A few weeks later, around late November, early December time, Barney asked if I was interested in having a trial with Leeds United, over in England. Again, I had never heard of Leeds. I asked what level they played at and was told they were in the second division, a reasonable standard by all accounts. Barney further explained that another black South African footballer played for the club, Gerry Francis, who had done well and made a decent name for himself there. I think it was Barney who had first introduced Gerry to Leeds. He said he had a good contact at Leeds, and with the support and input of Gerry Francis, the club had expressed a desire for me to go over for a three-month trial period.

There was one problem, I would have to part fund the flight and travel to Leeds myself! The club was prepared to put me up and feed me when I got to Leeds. They would give me a wage to cover my costs when I was there, but that really was as far as their commitment went. The upside was that if my trial was successful and they signed me, then I would be reimbursed for all my costs and they would pay for my return journeys to and from South Africa from Leeds, twice a year. There would also be a substantial wage for me to consider!

It was typical of me, nothing in my life was straight forward, I realised that the money for the flight was going to be an issue. Inside, I felt that the whole thing was going to be unattainable since there was also the need for passport clearance by the authorities and they were very selective about who they issued those to.

Barney was great, he discussed the situation with my family and said that he would find some money to help get me there. He expressed a real belief that I had what it takes to be a professional footballer in Europe. Everyone was thrilled and excited, everyone except me that is. I remained nervous about leaving behind everything I knew, everything I had grown up with, my family, my friends, my country. It didn't matter who I discussed the situation with, I got the same response each time. They would scream with excitement, hug me, and tell me I had to go and chase my dream and that it would be a mistake not to seize such an opportunity. 'Go for it Albert, this is your big chance,' they would say.

Because I hadn't ever been caught by the authorities committing any kind of anti-establishment activity (I always kept my opinions and thoughts about the oppressive establishment to myself), the government authorised my travel to England, adding plenty of provisos into the agreement, including, not returning to South Africa destitute or with liabilities. I had to laugh at this as I was clearly destitute when I was leaving the country for a place where I didn't know anyone, and had no idea at what address or place I would be staying or living.

The Jan Smuts airport in Johannesburg, as it was then known, barely resembles the modern day airport that exists on the same site. This was the departure point for Albert, where his journey to London airport, better known as Heathrow began. The flight time was a long one, roughly 13 hours by the recently procured Boeing 707 jets, the journey included refuelling stops.

> I was scared by the thought of flying, but excited by what lay ahead. It was a huge wrench leaving South Africa behind, but this was a chance to see different cultures, to escape the victimisation and torture we endured and to show the world that the black people of South Africa were equals to every other race, in every way!
>
> As I boarded the plane, I was shaking with worry and sweating heavily in anticipation, I was concerned about the flight, and what awaited me in England. I was so pent up that I had to go to the toilet and was sick several times before the plane had even taken off. The cabin crew were good to me, they put me at ease and treated me very well.
>
> As a footballer, I was a bit of a novelty, and people genuinely seemed interested in speaking with me. It certainly helped me forget that the jet was taking off, and before I knew it we were airborne and several thousand feet above South Africa. It felt very strange, unreal and dreamlike. It had happened so quickly and I wondered if I was doing the right thing. I had assured my family that I would return as often as I could, and I would write to them whenever it was possible.
>
> Sitting on that aeroplane I went through every emotion possible: elation, sadness and fear. I thought back to some of the things that had already happened in my life, I couldn't help it, I cried.

Jenny was one of the people in Johannesburg who I spoke with about Albert, she knew Albert and had actually been at the airport to see him leaving South Africa. It was back in January 1961.

> Albert looked so sad when I saw him at the airport, it wasn't at all the image of a man starting out in search of

a new life and looking forward to the exciting journey. I commented to my husband that it looked for all the world, that if he could run away from it all, he would. He didn't look confident at all, more frightened and unsure, he would occasionally smile, but was looking down at the ground for much of the time. It was as though he was scared to make eye contact with anyone.

There were many people there to wish him well, I think he may have been a little overawed that people cared for him. In hindsight, it must have been a daunting prospect for him, not many people in the Wintersrand knew or understood life beyond Germiston and the townships, and when you consider that he didn't know anyone in Leeds or England, it must have been terrifying for him.

Everything that he achieved, success or failure, was now going to be down to him, it was a new type of responsibility for him to deal with. I recall him clutching in his hand an old brown suitcase, and my thought at the time was that it probably contained everything (family excepted) that was important in his life. Finally, after going through all the official checks, he turned and waved to us all, and walked on, disappearing from our world for a whole new world and life elsewhere.

# 3

# Welcome to Leeds

Don Revie is often referred to and regarded as the man who brought and introduced Albert Johanneson to Leeds United. Nothing could be further from the truth. At the time, Revie was a highly respected player and no more, he had no influence in bringing Albert to Leeds for a trial.

A lot of people say to me that Mr Revie was the man behind my joining Leeds, they are wrong. In fact when I got here he was a player and then, he rarely spoke to me. He was very professional about his game and expected others to be the same, work hard in training and throughout games. I admit, I didn't like him when I first arrived, he had an arrogant sort of way about him, an aloofness that made him different to many of the other players. No one back chatted him, it was as though people were in awe of him. He was so much bigger than I was, and even when I was stood in front of him, he would talk over my head, ignoring my presence.

I felt that as a player he had little time for trialists, since they came and went, and in his mind why bother making friends or getting to know someone if they were not going to be about for long.

My own view was, he didn't like me, or didn't see it as his role to like me or interact with me, that was the manager's position. I was a trialist from another country, he wasn't interested in South Africa or what was happening there, and as I was not a first teamer I really didn't exist on his football radar. He wasn't alone in keeping a distance, initially, other players tended to ignore my presence and concentrated on themselves and getting into the manager's good books to get a chance at first team football.

So it was, that on Thursday, 5 January 1961, Albert Louis Johanneson arrived at London airport on the western extremities of England's capital city. It was cold and wet. London had experienced consistent rainfall since the turn of the year, with several inches falling across the city just a couple of days prior to Albert's arrival.

> I remember getting my first glimpse of England as the aeroplane began its descent towards London. From above, there was nothing but an expanse of green fields stretched out as far as I could see. I hadn't seen so much green land, ever.

When the plane eventually touched down and came to a standstill at the passenger concourse, Albert took his first steps on the Promised Land, passing through the customs checks without any hitch or delay.

> I felt very different walking through London airport, I didn't sense the animosity that existed in Johannesburg, yet the people walking around, going about their daily business, were clearly concerned by seeing a black man. I felt like I was on display and wasn't really sure what I was to do.
>
> In South Africa I would have been beaten and abused for being in such an environment alongside white people. Now it was different, whilst no one said anything offensive, the looks they gave me certainly didn't make me feel comfortable or welcome. I was extremely nervous and not really sure how to react, so kept my eyes fixed to the floor, occasionally glancing up to try to see some representative from Leeds United.
>
> It was at this point that I realised I had no idea how I would know who I was looking for, or meeting. I needed

to take stock of the situation so stopped and had a look around to see if I could see anyone who looked as though they might be looking for me. I had hardly put my suitcase on the ground when I was knocked forward with a hefty blow from behind me, I almost fell over. I turned to look at the cause and saw a tall burly looking man, dressed in a long overcoat and hat. 'Get out of my way nigger' he said, brushing down his coat with his hand, as though it might be contaminated with something nasty that had been caught through contact with me.

I apologised to him, but received no reply, only a further dirty look. I wanted to turn round and get back on the plane to Johannesburg. I was lost in a different part of the world, a world ruled by white people, very few of whom liked black people or saw us as equals. Inside I began to cry. I questioned whether coming to England was the right thing to do.

One can only imagine how difficult that situation must have been for Albert, tears rolled down his cheeks when he recalled the incident, the hopes and aspirations he held for a new bright future were put in perspective by the crass racist attitude displayed by the bully at the airport. The new world he had been told of and believed in, was not the place he imagined.

I don't deny that incident hurt, it shattered my illusion of a better world, yet as with many things in life, there was a positive side to it. I must have looked scared and lost, because a woman who had presumably seen and heard what happened, came up to me and asked if I was okay. She touched and stroked my arm in a sympathetic way. Never before had a white person touched me in a caring manner and I didn't know how to respond. I nodded in appreciation of her help and moved away. It was all very confusing for me.

Then I heard someone calling my name, 'Mr

Johanneson, Mr Johanneson.' I looked at a sea of white faces in an attempt to identify who it was that called me. I was feeling very nervous and vulnerable and wanted to get out of that wretched place as soon as I could. If this was what London offered, then forget it, my first impression of that place wasn't a good one.

A tall thin looking man with a beaming smile stepped forward, his hand outstretched towards me. 'Mr Johanneson, my name is Syd Owen, I'm from Leeds United football club, may I welcome you to England. Can I call you Albert?' he said. It was a relief if not a bit overwhelming to receive such a positive greeting after the earlier incident.

I told the man he could call me Albert as my name was Albert Louis Johanneson. He proceeded to bombard me with questions, ranging from how the flight was, to whether I was tired and hungry. It was all a bit too much for me, never before had a white person engaged me in so much conversation, certainly, no white man had ever concerned himself about my needs.

I was taken outside the airport to a waiting car which drove us into London. Soon, we were on our way to Leeds.

Albert's hope of a life of equality in Britain was based upon a dream, and unbeknown to him various political movements had already been created and publicly promoted a pro-white belief. In 1961, London had an estimated 100,000-plus Caribbean people living in its boroughs. The majority of these immigrants were given homes in slum and deprived areas, one such area of that time being Notting Hill. In that district, poverty, crime and violence were an accepted part of everyday life.

On the night of Friday, 29 August 1958 a gang of white youths had witnessed a Swedish woman arguing with her Jamaican husband outside Latimer Road underground station. The youths couldn't resist it and shouted racist comments and verbally abused the black man (Raymond

Morrison). To the group's horror, the Swedish woman (Majbritt) defended her husband and hurled abuse back towards them. They were angered that anyone would want to defend a black man and between them, resorted to get revenge.

The following evening they saw Majbritt Morrison and attacked her, using an iron bar, bottles, bricks and wooden batons. The police were called and safely escorted the poor woman home.

News spread that the authorities were taking the side of black immigrants versus white British people. This was the catalyst for public rioting, as later that evening, around 300-400 youths, mainly 'Teddy Boys,' gathered in the Notting Hill area, desperate for revenge. They made their way to Bramley Road, an area known to house many West Indian residents. What followed over the following six nights (until 5 September 1958) was bedlam, as mass rioting took place across the district, house windows were smashed, there was mass looting, street fighting and brawls everywhere as the authorities struggled to regain control of the area. Hundreds of people were injured in what was popularly known as the Notting Hill Race Riots.

Incredibly, the Home Secretary of the time, Rab Butler, refuted and denied all intimation that the riots were racially motivated, this, despite the fact that the majority of police officers on duty confirmed the basis that all the rioting had racial undertones!

As a result of the riots, in 1959 the Notting Hill Carnival was created, more as a pro-immigration statement than as any kind of celebration. Albeit, the black communities united and made a positive spectacle of the event.

Britain was a simmering pot of racial tension, and elsewhere, in 1958, the White Defence League (WDL), a far-right political group was formed. The WDL strongly opposed non-white immigration into Britain and were robust in the techniques they used to promote and convey that message. They sporadically produced their own newspaper 'Black and White News' and held regular marches and rallies across Britain. Gradually, support for their campaign began to emerge. In 1960 the WDL party joined forces with the National Labour Party and created a then newly formed British National Party. Later, on 20 April 1962, Adolf Hitler's birthday, the National Socialist Movement was formed as a splinter group from the British National Party.

If Albert Johanneson thought he was coming to a country where politics wasn't a bullying and oppressive tool, he was mistaken. Racial tension between all cultures was more evident in London than anywhere else, albeit, with an ever increasing stream of immigrants who were heading north, where property was easier to obtain and the overall cost of living and the economy was cheaper. Britain was in the grip of Conservative rule with Prime Minister Harold Macmillan infamously telling the nation that they had 'never had it so good,' and speaking of the perils of inflation. Not too dissimilar in content and views to speeches delivered by more modern Conservative party leaders.

> We took the train to Leeds and I was amazed by the views from the windows, fields of green, hills, trees, cars, the houses and towns we passed through looked nothing like Germiston or Johannesburg. There was nothing similar to the township, everything was so different from what I was used to.
>
> A man in the same carriage had a transistor radio, he was listening to song after song, it was a different type of music, but I liked what I was hearing through the crackly speaker. It was first time I had ever heard of Cliff Richard or heard his music. Imagine, not having heard of Cliff Richard seems ridiculous really, doesn't it? Yet this was

how starved of information we were in South Africa.

As it happens, Cliff was number one in the music charts in England at the time I arrived here, with a song called *I Love You*. I quickly established details about music and immediately thought that a decent transistor radio would be my first investment if I signed professional terms at Leeds.

I asked Syd and my other travelling companions as much as I could about the town of Leeds, I was corrected and informed that it was a 'city' and never to refer to it as a town as this would be seen as an insult by the local people. I was also told that Leeds people were regionally regarded as 'loiners.' I could only wonder whether this was a derogatory term or not?

There was so much I needed to learn and understand and from the outset, it was difficult educating myself to engage with the white people travelling the same journey and route as I was. A lifetime of being subservient and withdrawn had to be forgotten, it was now being made clear to me that I could talk and involve myself in discussion with all people.

As we approached Leeds station, I could see the built-up areas of the city, old and very proud looking buildings that looked down oppressively on gloomy streets below. My first impressions through the train window, was that it looked a grey and chaotic kind of place. I could sense my nerves as my stomach twitched with excitement and fear.

Grabbing my things, I moved towards the carriage door, wondering what the world on the other side was going to be like. The door opened and I felt a blast of cold air hit me, it was cold like I had never before experienced and I shivered. The station platform was busy with people rushing from the train towards the station exit, where they were greeted by their respective partners, loved ones and business contacts. I stepped down from the carriage and onto the platform, nervously taking my first steps away from the train and being ushered and told by Syd to 'hurry up or we'll miss our lift.'

As we moved through the station, which bears no resemblance to how it looks now (1991), I was shaking, not through nerves but through the cold and dampness of the place. Syd was dashing ahead of me continually reminding me to 'keep up Albert, come on lad, let's get to our car.'

Outside the station, we turned left and walked towards a waiting black car, which was by the Queens Hotel. The driver opened the door for me and called me sir, it was the first time in my life that a white person had addressed me so, it felt strange and I wasn't certain how to respond. The car moved through the city streets until we arrived at Elland Road. I could see the tall floodlights of the ground and felt so overwhelmed by my situation that I couldn't speak. The car pulled up outside the stadium and Syd paid the driver for our journey.

Everything was a whole new experience and I stood not knowing what to do while Syd chatted to various people who came up to him. I wasn't certain who they were, but none acknowledged my presence and that left me feeling a little sceptical of the welcome that awaited.

In an interview with Syd Owen in 1996, I asked him of his recollections of Albert on the day he arrived and joined the football club.

He was like a fish out of water, a scared rabbit caught in headlights to be honest, he had no idea what to expect or how he was going to deal with anything at all. I've never before seen anyone so lost and scared. Gerry Francis was another black footballer we had on our books who came from South Africa. He was very different to Albert, much more socially competent and able to hold his own in discussions and conversations.

Albert was much more withdrawn and quiet, but I could see he had an inquisitive side to him, and I realised that once he had got an understanding of what was expected of him, he would develop. The problem was that we didn't have the time to help new players and trialists integrate, it was down to them to establish roots and friendships.

Albert's bags were left with reception and as we walked through the club offices I told him he was going to meet Jack Taylor, the manager. I shall never forget Albert stopping dead in his tracks, looking at me with a bewildered sort of expression, he said, 'What is this person's name again, how am I to address him?' I couldn't help but laugh to myself, Albert didn't seem to be aware of anything about Leeds United and he had never heard of Jack Taylor. I couldn't believe that he was telling the truth, I had never considered that he was totally ignorant of English football.

I snapped back at him because I thought he was being belligerent, 'Jack Taylor is the manager, you will always call him Mr Taylor and nothing else until he tells you otherwise.' I visibly saw Albert's shoulder hunch forward and a strange look of uncertainty cross his face. I shouldn't have spoken so sharply to him, but like little children, you just never know whether these trialists are pretending to be ignorant and rude, or they genuinely are without knowledge.

As we approached Jack's office, I saw that the door was closed, this was generally a sign that he was busy, maybe with someone or on the telephone. To anyone other than his staff team, that meant his office was out of bounds. I knocked and heard Jack shout, 'come in.' I told Albert to wait where he was since it wasn't protocol for playing staff to walk into Jack's office unannounced. The poor lad, he looked terrified, his eyes were wide and he was hopping from foot to foot.

I walked into the office and closed the door behind me. Jack was sat reading through some paperwork. I told him Albert Johanneson was outside. 'What's he like?' asked Jack. I explained how I wasn't certain that anyone could be so oblivious or naive about everyday life in England yet he seemed so charming and pleasant that I couldn't imagine that he was being rude. 'Okay, bring him in and we'll have a talk, we can get a feel for what he is about,' Jack said.

I opened the door and invited Albert inside and introduced him to the Leeds manager. Albert was the perfect gentleman, he called Jack 'sir' and had to be told not to do that as Jack preferred to be called 'boss' which led to Albert adding boss at least three times in every sentence, which was equally as irritating.

Jack sat Albert down and asked him how the journey to Leeds had been and explained the various club protocols. He was a stickler for getting things right and giving respect where it was due and wanted to make sure that Albert knew that if the chairman, Harry Reynolds approached him, he was to be polite and courteous and say absolutely nothing about what went on in the dressing room. It wasn't peculiar to do that, since it was Jack's belief that the boardroom and the dressing room were two independent and different places, he was the go-between for both, not the players!

Albert quietly sat there, hands on his knees and his back very upright. 'Are you alright son, you aren't saying a lot?' Jack asked. Albert seized the opportunity and blurted out. 'Where will I sleep, sir? Will I be sleeping, here in the stadium, sir? Where will I eat, boss? Will I be allowed out on my own, sir? I don't have any boots, sir, can I play in bare feet, sir?' Jack laughed and placed a reassuring hand on Albert's shoulder, 'We will sort all that out for you Albert, I want you to look at the stadium, get to know where everything is in the ground and then we will take you up to where you will be living while you are here. We have got another coloured lad here, Gerry Francis, have you heard of him at all? He's black as well, so you are not on your own. Okay?'

Albert's recollection of the initial encounter with Jack Taylor was somewhat different:

I was made to wait outside the manager's office for a long time, I could hear them laughing in the office and thought that the manager must be a friendly soul. The door opened and I was invited in to meet him. He was huge and looked down on me. I was told to sit down, and then he told me how I should act and behave when in England. He said he understood that it would be difficult for someone like me to settle in England, but he expected me to manage and to act like my white colleagues, and the white people of the city. He also told me that I wasn't to bother him with trivialities and quickly to familiarise myself with Leeds and the people of Leeds. 'The best way to understand and learn about Leeds is to listen and learn, once these people know who you are they will take to you, until then, you have to prove yourself to them and to me and to the football club. I want no trouble from you, do you understand? If I do have problems, you'll be on that aeroplane back to South Africa on the same day.'

I was worried and felt intimidated by him, the man who was laughing behind a closed office door wasn't the same man now stood before me. It wasn't the welcome I expected but then nothing in my life had ever been easy. I understood that he wanted me to know how it was and where I stood, I had hoped that there would be a period of learning, but there wasn't, I was being thrown straight into it and life in Leeds.

I went for a wander around the stadium and a few people asked who I was and what I was doing there. I explained I was on trial from South Africa and they were then happy for me and shook my hand.

One man, a supporter, took me on an unofficial tour of the outside of the stadium, he was full of knowledge and very helpful to me getting to know where the parts of the stadium were to avoid during games, the areas where I would be called names. He said to me 'We have another blackie here, he's called Gerry Francis. Do you come from the same village out there?' I knew he wasn't being nasty or funny, he was just ignorant and stupid. I think he thought we lived in mud huts! Mud huts would be preferable to some of the houses back in South Africa. My first impression of England was that most people saw us different, they didn't think we had feelings or could be hurt by words and comments. I wasn't confident enough to speak out and put them in their place, yet they felt it okay to talk down to me. Mind you, it was in itself, a shocking experience to be acknowledged without taking a physical beating from a white man.

I returned to the club entrance and asked to see the boss, I was kept waiting for ages before he came out. He was smiling and put a fatherly arm around my shoulder and walked back into the offices. 'Listen, Albert, you are here on trial, that gives you certain rights, part of that is to be able to come and go as you like. You can walk through reception and into the players' areas, the dressing and treatment rooms. You don't have to ask, just do it, be a man and make your own decisions.'

He led me on his own tour of Elland Road football stadium, recounting his time in football and showing me the various terraces and seating areas of the ground. I asked him if blacks and whites stood and sat together in the stadium. He laughed, 'Yes they can and do, but we don't have that many black people here Albert, I rarely see one in the city. You are unique not only in Leeds, but across the entire football profession here in Britain. It's not going to be easy for you to integrate, I can name maybe half a dozen black footballers who play professionally here.

Many white people have a fear about your kind of people coming here, they will see you as being very different to them. Someone has already asked me if you are a witch doctor. I have put that person straight and in his place, he won't speak so irresponsibly again. Your colour is going to be a real problem Albert, just don't let the bigots get to you, rise above the criticism about your skin colour, there's nothing wrong with you, you are an equal here as far as I and all the players and staff are concerned, but you will have to deal with rudeness and ignorance yourself. I cannot be there shielding you 24 hours a day. Don't ever retaliate with violence, just rise above it, let your football skill be your response and do the talking for you, show them that you are better than them when it comes to the way they act.

The other thing you have to remember is, that you are representing Leeds United football club, that's my football club, so don't do anything that could ever put the name and integrity of the club into question. If you do, we will come down on you like a ton of bricks, okay.

Enjoy yourself, relax and show me what you can do with a football, if you make the grade and I think you are what we are after then there will be a career here for you. I will introduce you to Gerry Francis, he's a black footballer too, and a good person to get to know, he'll keep you right, Albert lad.'

Those words really helped me focus on what was expected of me, it was clear that even the boss hadn't any idea how life in South Africa was, and how that daily oppressive bullying and treatment that we suffered, affected black people. After this talk, I was taken to 13, Noster Hill in Beeston, where I would be living during my stay at Leeds. It was a very nice brick house, terraced and a short walk down the hill to the stadium.

The streets and houses nearby were all terraced and back to back it was a grey sort of area, yet I got to enjoy walking down Noster Street and down the steep grass hill that dropped down into more houses and finally out into Elland Road. I got to know the people in the area and that green hill at the end of Noster Street was luscious and felt like sponge under my feet. I would often stop and sit down there, looking out over Leeds city; it is a very powerful view and place.

The house at number 13, where I stayed, was a football clubhouse, and I it was here that I was first introduced to Edna Wineley, who was the landlady of the house. She was very much a caring woman, a person with a lovely smile and a manner that instantly put me at ease.

At first I was a little worried about my circumstances, it felt as though I was being watched and my movements monitored all the time, but I soon learned that unless it was something really bad that would affect us or the club, then this wasn't the case. She was there to help and guide each of the young footballers staying there. I recall the first words Edna spoke to me: 'My, we need to fatten you up young man, get some muscle put on your bones. Get your bags unpacked and I'll put the kettle on for a hot drink. Will it be tea or coffee for you?'

I hadn't tried tea that often, so I asked for a coffee and was shocked when she responded by asking 'Black or White?' It had to be explained to me that she meant with or without milk. We all laughed about the remark, it wasn't offensive at all but for a moment it surprised me.

I was then shown to my bedroom where I unpacked the few belongings I had brought with me in my suitcase. Nothing, and I mean nothing could have prepared me for the cold and the weather. It was a dreadful shock to my system. After sorting out my room, I sat on my bed and wondered what I was to do next. My legs felt tight and stiff and my back was hurting after all the travelling, so I elected to loosen myself up and go for a run to release the tension in my muscles. I also thought it would be a help in getting me warm as well as getting to know the district.

I didn't have a lot of clothes or footwear with me, one pair of shoes I think, and an old pair of football boots. I decided to go out barefoot, since this was most comfortable for me and the streets of Leeds were paved, not with gold, but concrete slabs, but there was also plenty of green fields around Noster Hill so I had choices of where I could run.

As I stepped out of the house on my own for the first time, I immediately sensed that Leeds was nothing like back in the township of Witwatersrand. The cold air and greyness of this area of the city gave it a depressing feel, it felt uncared for, unloved almost. I don't think the people who lived there realised how lucky they were to have such

The Driehoek Stadium, Germiston where Albert
watched games and often played

Revie's first signing. Albert
joins Leeds United in 1961

Leeds United
team photo
1962-63

Pre-season photo 1963
© Varley Picture Agency

Marrying Norma in Leeds

Cold, winter night action, cuffs pulled in
© Varley Picture Agency

Pre-match warm up in 1965

Albert and
colleagues enter
Wembley stadium.
FA Cup Final 1965

Hat-trick hero Albert
nets against Spora
Luxembourg
© Varley Picture Agency

Match action 1966
© Varley Picture Agency

Swivelling those hips
in training

Rare match action
image of Albert 1969

Albert in flow

© Varley Picture Agency

Relaxed for pre season training 1969

Albert lining up for York City 1970

Hitherto unpublished image of Albert playing
for Glenville FC (South Africa) 1973
Photo courtesy District Six Museum, Cape Town

fine homes with private walled gardens or backyards.

I turned right out of the house and made my way along the main road and soon passed a churchyard and burial ground with headstones. Everything was on a hill, and for the first time since arriving in Leeds, I could see around me hills and beautiful rambling countryside, it was quite an experience seeing it all for the first time. I did want to stop to take in the splendour of it all, but it was far too cold, so I continued my run.

I dropped down a narrow lane and a hill that led me down to a railway line and then cut through back to Elland Road. From here, I could see the football stadium from a different view. I was now looking towards the back of the big grandstand where the club offices were. I kept running along the pavement, past the football ground and then turned right through more narrow streets before running back up a grassy hill, which took me back to Noster Street and then Noster Hill.

It wasn't a long distance, but at least it warmed me up and my body felt a whole lot better now I had given it some exercise. I had also got to know some of the area so I felt a bit more comfortable in my surroundings.

Walking back into the warm house, I was greeted by Edna, I always called her Mrs Wineley and she would reprimand me for being so formal with her, but I thought I was being respectful. 'Albert, where have you been, where are your shoes, you must be freezing cold?' I was, the cold chilled me to my bones and my feet felt like blocks of ice. Edna seemed very concerned and said, 'Get yourself into a hot bath and never again go out in your bare feet, you will do yourself damage on those streets. If you hurt your feet you'll never get to play for Leeds United, and that won't do at all Albert.' I did as I was told and felt refreshed and warmed by the positive effects of the hot water.

I didn't like the weather and none of the clothes I owned were suitable for the climate. I needed things that would keep me warm, not the flimsy items I owned, but I had very little money immediately to be able to sort out

113

my wardrobe.

After settling down in the house, I was given dinner. Never before had I eaten and been prepared such a meal, it was like a banquet, there was hot meat, potatoes and peas and tea, lots and lots, of tea. Through Edna, I became a huge fan of tea and would take in several cups a day. After the meal I helped clear everything away and returned to my room where I laid on the bed. It had been an exhausting and emotional journey, it was a long way from Germiston to Leeds, but finally, I had arrived.

I felt relieved that for the time being at least, the travelling was over. It meant that I could concentrate on what I had come to England for, to play football and earn a professional contract and living. I had only been away for a day or so, yet I missed all of my family terribly. In those early days Leeds seemed such a miserable place, cold, dank and depressing. I missed the sunshine and the warmth created by knowing your surroundings and boundaries. I questioned whether I would ever be able to live in England, a place where black people were a rarity and clearly, in parts, not welcome. At least in the Wintersrand I had black people around me, people I could turn to and trust, people who understood how it felt to be called vile names and physically and mentally hurt by fellow human beings all because of skin colour.

# 4

# Three Months – It Felt Like Three Years!

Standing at five foot seven inches and weighing in at 10 stone, Albert was anything but an imposing figure, he may have been small in stature, but he was big in heart and desire. In coming to England and Leeds for a trial, he had a point to prove, not only to himself and to those back home in the Wintersrand, but to British football too.

> I knew I was capable and had the ability, yet my future lay with white people, I was now living in a white man's world and the differences I had to cope with were more than cultural.
>
> I don't think I slept a wink that first night in Leeds, it was so cold and outside it seemed like a different world to me. The housing estate around Noster Hill was oppressive. Whenever I looked out of my window, all I could see everywhere was rooftops and even more houses, and it seemed so dark all the time. I was awoken early and told to wash and dress later. Downstairs, I was presented with a big breakfast. I wasn't used to such a fuss and so much food being available.
>
> After breakfast I made my way to the Leeds United football stadium, it was easy to spot and find, it sat at the bottom of a hill a couple of streets behind Noster Hill. As I walked into the ground, I felt my nerves kick off. I was unsure how I would treated and greeted by the rest of the players.

One of the first people Albert met was fellow South African, Gerry Francis.

What a good man he was, he welcomed me with a huge hug and a beaming smile, I was reassured by this and Gerry told me he would show me the ropes and introduce me to the rest of the players and give me the heads up on who does what and the unwritten protocols of the club, of which there were many. He explained that the vast majority of the people at the club were kind and understanding, but there existed an element that was not so forgiving or accepting of certain people, especially those with a different colour of skin. Gerry advised me to take everyone at face value and to form my own opinion on individuals. It was good advice.

One of the genuine characters of the team was a lad called Peter McConnell, he was full of fun and mischief and sometimes, when he spoke to me, I wasn't certain whether he was being serious about something or if he was having fun. He too seemed a decent sort of person, he was very confident and not at all afraid to express his own opinions. Unfortunately, as a footballer he wasn't as skilful or adaptable as many others I saw. Rigid and ruthless, is probably a good description of how he was as a player, there was little artistry to his game, which could be an asset in training matches since he never held back in a challenge and many of the players would avoid going into the tackle with him.

Peter had a wonderful attitude, a 'never say never' sort of manner, defeat and loss were not things he would accept so it was always good to be on the same side as he was. I admired his toughness. Don't get me wrong, he was no thug, just strong and reliable, both as a player and in his everyday life.

Peter was always courteous to me although I'm not absolutely certain that sometimes he knew how to take me. I was shy and quiet and did my utmost not to get involved in other people's business. A football club is like any other place of work, there was always talk going on here and there; gossip and rumours flying about. It's part of life really and footballers are no different from any other human being, they have weaknesses and insecurities and, as most people do, they like to be in the know because knowledge is power.

The initial thing that struck me on my first day at Leeds United, was the collective attitude of the players, they all wanted to be part of the club and do well for themselves as a unit and the supporters too. I learned from Billy Bremner how important the fans are to any football club, not only because they pay valuable money into the club but through their loyalty and passion. It genuinely inspires players to hear the crowd and fans getting behind the team or them as individuals. No matter what any footballer may say, we do hear what the crowd and individuals shout out, sometimes it hurts, sometimes it motivates you to give more.

This camaraderie and spirit became much more obvious when Mr Taylor or one of his staff was around, it was as though some of the lesser quality players felt the need to display their own loyalty to the group in order that he could witness it. They were trying to influence him. It was a peculiar sort of behaviour that I had never before come across. Later, I learned these players were ingratiating themselves so that they may gain favour from him and get a shout at first team football. It goes without saying, that those acting this way were not first eleven regulars, probably not even in the top fifteen at the club.

From day one it became clear that there was a seniority order to everything, some players could get an audience with Mr Taylor, others, like myself, couldn't. Not that I wanted to involve myself in any of the internal politics, I needed to prove my value and worth with a football and show my new colleagues that my performances and skills could further enhance the team, before I considered myself able to settle down to anything else.

I felt embarrassed when I saw the players dressing into

old training kit, I didn't know whether to just take a kit or wait until someone offered me something to wear.

I didn't even have my own boots to play or train in, the club trainer noticed my reticence to help myself to kit, and helpfully gave me some items and a used pair of Adidas three striper boots that belonged to the football club. When I say used, they were almost like new, better than anything I had ever put on my feet before. I was told that it would be my responsibility to look after them, clean them and to keep the leather soft.

When I first put the boots on it felt like someone had bound my feet in rope, they were uncomfortable because they were not what I was used to: bare feet. I had no sensation of touch in them, it was a bit like poking at a football with a stick to begin with. I spoke to Gerry about it and he told me that I should wear them as often as I could, until they felt like my hand in a well fitting glove. He explained because of the British weather I would need to know how to use them to aid my surface grip, turning and getting a standing start when setting off on a sprint or a run, and importantly, ball control.

Initially the boots felt terrible, and I still remember a ball being kicked to me and my effort to return the pass to the player. I had the touch and control of a rhinoceros and apologised to everyone for looking so stupid. Billy Bremner thought it hilarious and said I was walking as though I had lead diving boots on my feet. I confided in him that I wasn't used to playing in boots. He asked what I generally played football in if it wasn't boots, and when I told him that I played in my bare feet he looked horrified and laughed. He thought I was kidding!

Billy was a good man, a great man even, he understood that I needed help, so took me to one side and explained the best ways to 'wear a boot in' so it became comfortable. I still remember him saying to me on that initial day, 'Al, your feet will earn you your living, you must protect and look after them, always keep them in good shape. I hear from Gerry that you are an inside forward and you have magic in your feet, we don't have that many players here who are like that, if you are to do well here then you must have the best you can get. If your boots aren't right then tell someone, but for heaven's sake, don't try to play or train in bare feet, you'll hurt yourself, and don't be surprised if someone doesn't stamp on them and damage them. They won't do it deliberately, but we have a few carthorses here, good at certain things but not others. When they go into the tackle they aren't at all careful, we all have cuts and bruises from our training sessions, if something like that happens to your feet then it will be the end of your time here. So be sensible Al, don't be scared to speak out, just ask one of us, someone will help you, we are all in this together, a team.'

I thought to myself, what a pleasant young man, he carries no prejudice towards me and I feel comfortable in his company, it was a rousing chat that made me feel welcome.

When I told Gerry about it, he further confirmed that Billy was one of the best people at the club. Yes, he was brash, noisy and loud, but his heart was in the right place and he knew how difficult it was for new people coming into the football club, especially from other countries.

Billy had come down to Leeds from Scotland, which, as far as I was concerned may have been in the Arctic Circle. He had struggled to settle in and missed his homeland. His accent was very different to the Yorkshire dialect I had already picked up. I initially struggled to understand what he was saying and wondered if that would be a problem people had with me and my South African English?

An hour or so later, after running and a few workouts, I was facing Billy on the training pitch. I saw him as a new friend so didn't feel threatened or intimidated by him, though it did feel strange competing against and alongside white men. It didn't seem to bother my team mates that I was black, they treated me like any other player.

The first time I got the ball it was a pass. I controlled it and looked up to see Billy approaching. I went to push it past him and run around the outside, up the wing. As I moved to sidestep him he clattered straight into me, he somehow used his hip as a lever and flipped me into the air. I went sprawling into the cold and muddy wet grass of the training pitch. I wasn't certain what to do, it hurt and I was filthy, but it was my pride that hurt more than anything physical. Everyone was laughing and made comments such as 'welcome to Leeds' or 'enjoy your Bremner mud bath.' It was all lighthearted and no malice was intended or taken. I got up, brushed myself down and moved away from Billy, since I realised he was the competitive sort and would want to win every challenge, especially against me, the new kid.

I found room to receive the ball, again it was cleared by the defence up to me. This time, before I even touched it, someone clattered straight into the back of me, and again I was sent sprawling to the ground and into the mud. I was frustrated because I wasn't getting a chance to show my skills, I wanted to say something but feared further reprisals and heavy tackles. When I looked up to see who my aggressor was, it was Billy, and he was laughing. He offered me his hand and pulled me back to my feet. 'I thought you were a speed merchant Al? You need to be a lot quicker than that to get past me,' he said with a wink, as he trotted off again in search of the ball.

This action went on each time I got the ball or went anywhere near it, someone, normally Billy, would take me out of the game. I was so frustrated and getting quite anxious that Mr Taylor and his staff were watching and would think me totally useless. I wanted to show him and my new colleagues how skillful I was, yet I wasn't being allowed the opportunity to do anything. It was a tough lesson I was learning, life at Leeds wasn't going to be easy, I would have to work hard and find alternatives to avoid the clattering challenges.

Another player who was playing in my side, a left back called Grenville Hair, walked up to me and told me to drop deeper towards him and to go wide left, as this would allow me a bit of additional time and freedom to escape the boots and studs of Billy Bremner. I did as he asked, and immediately received a pass from him that gave me the opportunity to run with the ball. I swept past a couple of half hearted challenges and looked up to see if I could centre the ball to someone with a better goalscoring opportunity. Then I saw the form of Billy Bremner thundering towards me. He was charging at me like a steam train. I waited until he had committed himself to the challenge, and gently lifted the ball over his outstretched leg and skipped passed his sliding body, leaving him behind in the mud. I heard him shouting at me, 'Al, you bastard.' I didn't hang about to hear anything else he said, I squared the ball for John McCole to score. It felt good, great even, I wasn't certain whether to celebrate, what to do or what to say really, and no one said anything extra special to me, other than 'well played Albert.'

I had been forced, through tactics to play outside left, and I confess I felt comfortable in that position, it was Grenville Hair who played me into that position. His vision and passing into space was influential in helping me bed into the squad during training sessions.

As my confidence grew, I managed to score a couple of goals myself in that initial training session. I knew deep down that training session goals meant nothing and alone, would not win me a contract at the club, there was much more to being a professional footballer at Leeds United, it was the complete package they looked at, how I was as a person and how I led my life on and off the pitch.

After training, I waited behind for everyone else to leave. Despite doing reasonably well I felt disappointed with my overall pace and ball control, I felt that the boots were more of a hindrance than an asset and I knew I had to improve consistently it if I was to impress Mr Taylor, so decided to work as hard as I could to develop my game.

I spoke with the groundsman, a man by the name of Cecil (Burrows) I think, and asked if he minded if I stayed out on the training pitch and did a bit more training. He said he didn't mind as long I didn't churn up any more of the grass as it was a bit of a mess. My feet were really uncomfortable, so I removed the boots and trained in my bare feet. I thought this was a good choice since I wouldn't damage the grass or my feet. I worked with the ball and my control of it for about an hour, before the groundsman came out and told me to go to the changing rooms as he now needed to work the pitch.

When I turned to leave the training pitch there was a small crowd stood watching. They were fans and they applauded me. I felt honoured that they enjoyed my performance. It reminded me of the time I entertained people in Germiston with my football skill with a tennis ball.

As I got near the crowd they approached and surrounded me and asked for my autograph, never before had I been asked by a group of so many people to sign autographs. I remember one young boy asking me, 'Who are you? We already have a blackie at the club you know.' I smiled at him and told him my name was Albert Louis Johanneson, I was from South Africa and I wanted to play for Leeds United. This was met with many handshakes and the people seemed happy to hear that from me.

One man shouted out to a group of others who were nearby, 'Here lads, that darkie fellow from the South African jungle is here, come and take a look.' I felt a lump appear in my throat, that comment hurt me and put me straight back to feeling inferior and a lesser being than the gathered white people were. I know the comment wasn't meant to hurt me, it was a stupid and non intelligent remark caused by lack of education, but really that was no excuse. I didn't hang about and returned to the dressing room before I heard anything else that might upset me.

The dressing room was empty, the majority of the players had gone home, so I sat down on one of the benches and looked around me. I wasn't certain if this was what I expected or wanted, it had been a difficult initiation and although my colleagues didn't treat me any differently, it was obvious from the supporters' comments that the people of Leeds did see me as different. I put my head in my hands and began to cry, I was sobbing and felt so alone. Through my tear-filled eyes I saw someone's feet stood in front of me. I felt very foolish and vulnerable knowing that whoever this person was knew I was upset and had been crying. When I looked up it was Grenville Hair, looking very smart and dapper in his casual clothes. I stood up and apologised immediately, telling him I was sorry for being upset and acting like a baby.

Grenville sat me down and reassured me that he didn't see me as a baby, nor did anyone else. 'For what it's worth, I thought you were the best player in training today, Albert,' he said, and hearing this greatly cheered my spirits and mood. 'I've not seen anyone cause Billy to miss a tackle and leave him behind like you did out there. Nobody may have said anything at the time, but we were all impressed by that, none more so than Billy himself, but be warned, he has sworn to get his revenge on you.'

This comment worried me, as I thought I must have upset Billy, however, Grenville explained to me that Billy could be a heap of troublesome fun and anything he would do to get his revenge, would be in good spirits and not harmful, hurtful or disrespectful. 'Billy only hurts people he plays against and who aren't Leeds, if you are part of this club then you are part of Billy, he doesn't ever hurt his own so don't worry yourself about it, just be aware he'll be watching and waiting,' he added, before walking out of the dressing room and saying he would see me tomorrow for the game!

That awareness of Billy Bremner initially kept me on my toes, I wasn't certain whether to apologise to him or to avoid him, then it dawned on me that I should just concentrate on myself and my own game, not on that of Billy Bremner or anyone else. I wondered what game Grenville referred to and whether it was Billy's game?

I leapt into the biggest bath I had ever seen. It was a communal bath which all the players shared after a game or training. I believed that they wouldn't want to share it with me, a black man! The water was lukewarm but it took the chill from my bones.

I was getting dressed when Mr Taylor entered the dressing room. 'Are you alright Albert?' he enquired. I told him I was and that I had stayed behind to do some additional training. 'Good, that's what I like to see Albert, it's good to train hard, you'll learn a lot from our players. In the main they are a great bunch, so when you go back to South Africa you will be a better player for all this experience. Be here tomorrow for 9:30 a.m., okay, we will do a bit of light training. We have a cup match tomorrow and it's a game I want us to win. You can come and watch, get a feel for what the English game is about, it's not all about speed, skill and running, it's about teamwork, tactics and being part of a unit and understanding and sharing a common goal. Our goal is success at all costs, for Leeds United.'

The initial part of his statement devastated me, it was my first full day at the club and already, Mr Taylor was telling me that I was going back to South Africa. As I walked back to Noster Hill, I was cursing myself for ever leaving South Africa. I genuinely believed that Mr Taylor had already made up his mind that I wasn't good enough. I felt angry that he could treat me, use me like this.

That evening I visited a church, St Mary's, it was just along the road from my house at Noster Hill. There I prayed that everything would come good for me and my family. I sat in a pew, crying and sobbing. It was then that I felt a reassuring hand on my shoulder. I looked up and saw a cleric before me. 'Are you okay my lad?' he enquired. I explained what Mr Taylor had said to me and how I missed my family for their support when things were tough for me. I expected a religious response, an explanation about how the church would support me and act as my family. It didn't happen. Instead the cleric explained to me that I was analysing everything too deeply, and taking everything too literally. He said that he knew Mr Taylor and that he was a good and fair man who wouldn't make a decision on one training session. I apologised for displaying weakness and after a few words of religious wisdom were conveyed to me, I left the church and returned to Mrs Wineley's.

Despite everything, I was so worried about my situation that I never slept a wink that night. The next day Leeds were playing in the Football Association (FA) Cup competition, at Sheffield Wednesday. It was a strange sounding name for an English football team, Wednesday, I had never heard of them.

When I got to the football stadium the following morning I felt rotten. I was so cold and it seemed to be getting colder by the minute. There was much activity taking place inside and outside of the ground, people rushing around doing things, and checking the playing kit.

Training wasn't at all like it had been the day before, for a start, there were fewer of us and it was all stamina based, lots of running and gym work that if nothing else, helped keep me warm.

Afterwards, as became my way, I stayed behind and allowed the other white players to take their bath first, I kept out of the way since I did not want to embarrass or offend anyone by taking my place for granted, nor did I want them to tell me to bathe alone. It was something I felt was best avoided.

I was kicking the ball about on the training pitch when someone from the club office came out and shouted for me to hurry up and get ready. I didn't know, but a few of us were travelling down to Sheffield by car to watch the game. I quickly bathed, dressed and in double quick time was ready, I got in the car with two office staff and another trialist.

When we arrived at the Sheffield Wednesday stadium (Hillsborough), I was greeted with nasty comments from people going to the game; it was abuse about my colour and my country. They were referring to me as a 'nigger boy' and asked if my colour washed off in the bath. It was an uncomfortable situation and I felt sorry for the people who were with me. I thought how embarrassed they must be, being seen with me in public.

The abusive comments didn't stop and I was relieved when we got to the officials' entrance. The officials I was with walked straight into the reception area, I was stopped by a man stood at the door, and told I wasn't welcome or allowed in that entrance. The man, a Wednesday official, refused to let me pass. Words were exchanged with others in the area, and I was left in no doubt that I was not going to be allowed access to the official areas of the club.

It was only after Billy Bremner had seen some fans that the matter was resolved. He came out and saw my anguished expression as I stood outside the entrance. He asked what was happening and why I wasn't inside with the rest of the players. I told him what had happened and pointed out the bully of a man who denied me access. Billy took it on his shoulders to explain to the man that I was a Leeds United player and had more right to be there than he did as a jumped-up security guard. He went bright red and was forced to relent and allowed me past and into the ground.

I have to confess that Billy wasn't polite to the man, nor could his words be misconstrued in any way. What he told the man was I was a Leeds United footballer and a personal friend and he didn't like anyone speaking to or treating his friends so badly. If he didn't let me in he would 'knock his block off.' He made him apologise to me for his rude behaviour. I was stunned, never before had a white person defended and protected me, and I wasn't at all certain how to deal with it.

It was a short respite, I may have got through the door and into the ground, but where we were sat, the abuse and negative comments about my colour continued throughout the game. The cynical white attitude felt every bit as oppressive as it did in South Africa, and I resigned myself that this was how life was for black people, no matter which country they lived in; white people believed they were the rulers and we were inferior.

The football I saw that day was extremely poor. It was my first taste of competitive football in England. It was a million miles from the style of play shown to us by Stanley Matthews and his colleagues, when his team toured South Africa.

I have to say that Leeds looked a very average side that day, and I wasn't impressed. Sheffield Wednesday ran out 2–0 victors, the only real difference between the teams being that Sheffield were much more physical and seemed stronger.

Throughout, I sat shivering, it was so cold that I thought my toes were going to drop off, the tip of my nose was numb and I could hardly move my jaw to speak. In those first few days, I wasn't at all endeared to Yorkshire or England, the weather in particular was a problem for me, and I wondered how the players endured such extreme temperature drops out on the pitch.

On the Sunday I revisited the local church, St Mary's in Beeston. So far as churches go, it was a wonderfully peaceful place for prayer. I stood gazing at the outside of the building with its grand windows and tower. I was reluctant to go inside as the vast number of people who entered were white and many looked at me with suspicious curiosity and I felt uncomfortable. I was a devout Christian and enjoyed my religion. I wanted to find spiritual strength to help me through my trial period. I needed support and the church, as I had already ascertained, seemed the right thing to turn to.

An old couple entering the building stopped and looked back at me, the man beckoned to me and invited me to come in and join them. The cleric must have heard them as he came out and invited me in. He took me by the arm and led me into the church and sat me down alongside other members of the congregation. It felt good, everyone was focused on the service, and no one treated me differently.

The unity among my Leeds United colleagues and that received from the church were very much two positives in my life in Yorkshire. After the service I walked back along Beeston Road towards Noster Hill. A group of young people were walking along the pavement towards me, they took up the entire width of the pavement and it was obvious to me that they were not going to give way.

Not wanting any kind of conflict I kept my eyes fixed on the floor and tried to squeeze through them. They wouldn't move and deliberately knocked into me with their shoulders and elbows, and wouldn't allow me to get past. I sensed danger and decided to turn round and walk back to the church with the group still following me. They were calling me a wog and a coconut head, and many other insults.

As I approached the front door of the church the vicar appeared. He had heard the commotion and came out to confront the group, asking them why they were challenging me in such an obscure way. One youth, a rather well built (fat) boy told him that people like me weren't welcome in England because we were different to them. 'It is the nigger's role to be treated badly, they expect it from us white people, after all, they were slaves' he proclaimed!

I'm not certain that clerics are supposed to lose their temper, but this gentleman did. He moved right into the centre of the group and said to them, 'What would you think if I told you this man is no different to you or I, and he is a footballer with Leeds United?'

The group's response surprised me. 'Leeds United are shit, no wonder they are shit when they have darkies playing for them.' The group mocked the vicar and told him his church would be burned to the ground for allowing a black witch doctor inside. They walked away. I felt confused and more than a little agitated by the attitude people were showing towards me. The vicar understood my concerns, and said to me, 'Ignore them, they are ignorant, they don't understand, you are always welcome here, we embrace all human beings and communicate one common language to all races.'

I thanked him for helping me and was about to leave when he asked if I would like him to walk me home? I told him I needed to get used to the area and the area needed to get used to seeing me, so it was better that I tried to deal with things and situations myself. He shook my hand and advised me to be careful, and I left.

I wasn't a violent person, I hated confrontation yet I knew that to succeed in English football I had to deal with conflict through the discrimination of everyday life in England. As I walked along Beeston Road I considered my situation and something inside told me that I was fortunate to be given such an opportunity and to embrace it as an opportunity for personal development and to show the world that black people and footballers were no different to anyone else.

I am a firm believer that everything happens for a reason. Here I was in Leeds, I had an opportunity to change my life, my background and skin colour wasn't a problem to me, if it was for others, then it was for them to resolve those issues. I was in Leeds to play football, many of the people I had met were so prejudiced against black people that I knew I couldn't change anything by talking to them. I had to somehow speak to them through a universal language we all understood, I would educate them through my football skills. If they saw that I was as good as any white player, then they might just accept me as their equal in life too.

\* \* \* \* \*

In today's diverse and multicultural society, it is difficult to appreciate how different and difficult everything must have been for Albert back in 1961. It cannot be put into any kind of perspective. However, imagine how it would feel being a human being on an alien planet, a place where you are deliberately made to feel uncomfortable, and in the main, unwelcome. That was not only Leeds but the England which Albert Johanneson, a brave young man from South Africa, had to live in on a daily basis. A lesser person suffering such abuse in what was a relatively short space of time, 48 hours, would have buckled under such pressure. In truth, had Albert elected to take that option, no one could have questioned his reasons for doing so. When I asked him how strong the temptation was to walk away from Leeds and his future in those first few days, he told me:

> Paul, I was in turmoil, in my bedroom I cried, I wanted so much to go home but knew that if I did that, then I would have let down my family and everyone in the township who had backed me and wanted me to succeed.
>
> I couldn't really talk to anyone about how I was feeling since I didn't trust anyone to know my inner self, I thought they would see how I felt as a weakness, nor did I feel able to tell them what was happening to me as it would highlight a problem that could easily be resolved by sending me back to South Africa. I didn't want that, I wanted a fair chance to prove myself an equal and good enough. If I could achieve that, then black South Africans and our style of football would be taken seriously, I was doing it for every black person at home in the townships and elsewhere across South Africa and the world. For every dozen or so rude people I encountered there was a further half dozen who were good, friendly and genuinely okay with me as a black man in a predominantly white country.

The following day Albert awoke to the greatest surprise of his life.

> I pulled back the sheets on my bed and was about to get out to get ready for breakfast and training, but I could

hear other people moving about in the house. It was dark outside. Then the cold hit me, it was bitter and I could see my breath as I exhaled. I looked out of a window but could see nothing; it was so cold that ice had formed from the condensation inside. I scratched an area of ice away and saw a white blanket of snow; it was still falling heavily outside. With it being so cold I thought there would be no training that day so got back into bed and tried to keep myself warm.

The next thing, there was heavy knocking on my bedroom door, it flew open and Syd Owen was stood there. 'Albert, what the fuck are you doing, get yourself up and out of there, we've got training in a bit, you'd better not be late. Come on, get up and get down the football ground as quick as you can.'

My heart was beating like it never had before, I rushed about, dressed and missing out on my breakfast, I went directly down to the ground. The snow on the ground was crisp yet it felt soggy beneath that. I jogged part of the way but was forced to take it steady. As I went down the hill the ground was slipping away from beneath my feet and I landed on my backside several times during the walk.

When I got to the ground, many of the players were already out training, I tried to be inconspicuous and sneak in without anybody noticing me, not easy as a black person in a truly white world. The players saw me, and collectively shouted out, 'Good morning Albert, did you enjoy your lie-in this morning?' I nodded and smiled back at them and quickly got myself changed.

Mr Taylor joined me as I was getting ready. 'Albert, did you have a good weekend, how are you settling in?' I told him I was surprised at how cold the weather was, and he followed this up by asking what I thought of the game against Sheffield Wednesday. I chose my words carefully, and said I had seen how physical Wednesday were in preventing Leeds from playing football.

Mr Taylor was an honest man and I was surprised at how candid his comments were to me. 'Albert, I have brought you over here because this football club needs players who know how to use a football and how to play the game. People like Jack Charlton, Grenville Hair, Freddie Goodwin, John McCole. They are good honest players who work hard for the club, they are solid and reliable. I tell them to do a job and they do it.

Players like Billy Bremner create opportunities that change games, you have that skill too, you can create. What I need to see from you is the passion, commitment and desire to do well for me and for Leeds United.

I thought we were rubbish at Sheffield, they outfought and outplayed us. Many of the players at this club are not up to the standard I demand, so I will make changes and bring fresh new young players in. I want you to be one of those Albert, show me you can meet my standards.

This is your first lesson Albert, always be honest about football, it's no good saying we did well if you know we were poor. If you have a shocker I'll tell you, if you play well, I'll applaud you and pat you on your back. There is little point in me telling you how good you are when in reality, you are shit. So always be honest about football, be honest with yourself, honest with your team mates and honest with the supporters.

The supporters in England will let you know how well or poorly you are playing, that's why it's important to always give of your best. That way, you'll earn respect and that's respect from the players as well, they'll be watching you all the time throughout your trial, seeing how you react to different things. Impress them with your attitude and you are on your way to winning a contract. I don't mean impress them with your ability to juggle a football. I mean impress them as a person and with your professionalism be first to training, be the last to leave, keep your own counsel and support them when you think it is right to do so. Be yourself Albert, don't try to be anyone else and trust me, you won't go far wrong.'

No one had ever spoken to me in such a way, from that moment on I had nothing but the utmost respect for Mr

Taylor. I wanted to please him, make him realise he had made a good decision in bringing me to Leeds United.

Unfortunately, I never really got the chance to sit down and talk with him again, results and team performances never improved, they were average to poor and the team sat in the lower reaches of the division in which they played.

The supporters weren't satisfied with his style of play and screamed their objections at him during games. I saw a change come over him, he always appeared preoccupied and desperate to get things right. He demanded more from the players and became openly critical of them. The more he pushed the players, the more I felt they pulled away from him.

There were certain unsettling elements within the dressing room, players who would say one thing to Mr Taylor and then say another behind his back. I often saw them speaking to club directors. That sort of damaging behaviour cannot have helped Mr Taylor's position.

I didn't want any involvement in the politics, I knew first hand from South Africa how destructive politics was. In the bigger scheme of things, internal politics are destructive and many of those involved in such activities have motives, they are often selfish and insecure, in putting someone or something else down; they falsely believe it reflects better upon themselves. From experience I know that such people are not to be trusted.

\* \* \* \* \*

Away from the club life began to improve for Albert, he began to settle into his new environment.

As I began to get an understanding of how life is in Leeds, I slowly started to get out and about a bit more, exploring the area and going into the city where life was far different from that at Beeston. I tried to find other black African communities in the city, but back then there were so few black people in Leeds that it was like searching for a needle in a haystack.

With my first money from Leeds, I bought a transistor radio, it was constantly playing in my room, and I would pretend to dance with imaginary partners to the music it produced. I loved music and dancing, it was very much part of how I saw my football skills, like a dancer, gliding past challenges, turning, twisting, fast then slow, calm then erratic. There are comparable forms of athleticism involved, but the music in England was the best.

Some of the other players would pull my leg a bit because I was always singing or humming to myself. Billy Bremner once told me he thought that the Johnny Tillotson number, *Poetry in Motion* could be about me when I was juggling with the ball at my feet. It was always on the radio along with different versions of *Rubber Ball* by Bobby Vee and Marty Wilde. Music and dance, all I needed was the romance!

It wasn't very long before I found myself being taken along to some of the more fashionable dancing clubs; the big band sound was all the rage and appealed to me with its range of music. I remember going to dances at places like Armley, Bramley and Pudsey baths and to different town halls. It was good to be able to mix and socialise in such places, we all had a common purpose, to dance and enjoy ourselves and it felt very good. I was still missing my home in South Africa and sent letters home with money for the family, I made calls whenever I could, but it was difficult with the time differences and coordinating such things was almost impossible with the distances involved.

On the football side of things, I was playing regular trial games and featuring with the first team in training. I felt that my skills were improving all the time and my confidence grew with each day that passed.

Gerry Francis and I got to know each other well, he was such a good human being and would go out of his way to help anyone. On one occasion we were walking along Elland Road and saw a tramp laid on the pavement.

Gerry stopped and asked him if he was okay, the man was drunk and could hardly speak, he stunk of stale alcohol and urine. He was filthy. It didn't matter to Gerry, he treated everyone with the same dignity, we somehow got the man up on his feet and walked (carried him) him to a seat. He seemed grateful, although he couldn't show it. He looked at me in such a way that I knew he wanted to say thank you but couldn't.

That was the kind of man Gerry Francis was. He introduced me to many different people in the city, people he thought would be helpful, understanding and supportive of me. It was very much a case of finding my own way in life and making my own relationships. Gerry would point me in the right direction but the hard work of making and maintaining friendships was down to me.

At the football club, like everywhere else, there were groups of people who stuck together, looked after each other and tended to socialise together. As a trialist, I wasn't accepted as part of the team, such privileges came with a playing contract.

Few trialists are accepted with open arms, you are initially seen by some as a threat to their position in the club. It's all about proving your worth, showing your merit and gaining trust. In the games I featured in, I think I did okay, certainly some of the supporters who would come down to watch us cheered me on. They seemed to like it when I ran at players and used my speed.

I told someone just once that in Germiston I was sometimes called Albert 'Hurry, Hurry' Johanneson. The name spread like wildfire and soon I was being referred to by the fans who saw me as 'Hurry, Hurry Johanneson'. I didn't really like the name, but many people thought it suited my style of play, so for a while it stuck.

I thought my time with Leeds was over when manager Jack Taylor suddenly left the club. It came as a bit of a surprise but I had noticed that things were getting a bit stale in training. He seemed less involved and withdrew himself from many of the things he had previously been involved in.

I was training on my own and had been working extra hard and since I was almost three months into my trial period and no offer of a contract had been made, I wasn't confident I would get one. I knew that if nothing happened shortly then I would be returning to the township in South Africa. It wouldn't be the end of the world if I had to go back, and although I knew that I had what it takes to be a success, unless the club and Mr Taylor made the offer, then it didn't actually matter what I believed.

It was our trainer, Les Cocker, who told me that Mr Taylor had resigned as manager. Les was another good man, his knowledge and awareness of fitness, stamina and football were the best I encountered during my time in the game. As a trialist, I would be one of the last to know what was going on behind the scenes at the club, so was probably one of the last to find out. Les shouted for me to stop training and called me over. I shall never forget his words. 'Albert, I expect you have heard the news? I'm sorry, I don't know what is going to happen with you, the manager has resigned and we don't yet know who is coming in to take charge. They will make a decision on your future and obviously, a new manager coming in isn't going to know anything about you. I will recommend you and I know Syd Owen will, but it's not our decision, I'm sorry Albert.'

I asked what I should do and whether I should return to South Africa and await contact. Les told me to go back to the clubhouse and to come back for training as usual the following day.

So much was going through my mind as I made my way back to the house, it seemed that fate had conspired against me and through no fault of my ability, I was going to miss out on a professional career in England. I was so sad and felt very alone in my thoughts. There was nothing I could do, so I went to church and prayed that all would be right for me and my family. I felt comfortable inside the church, it was always a wonderful place to take time out and consider life's options.

The atmosphere at the house and at the club in the aftermath of Mr Taylor's resignation was dreadful, everyone felt insecure about their future, even people like Les Cocker and Syd Owen had no idea what was going to happen. Gerry Francis told me he thought things would change and he believed he was on his way out anyway.

I remember Jack Charlton telling me not to worry, as I was a bloody decent footballer and an honest lad and he was sure that whoever came in would be interested in looking at me further. Peter McConnell was another who believed I would be okay in England, and whilst it was very nice having such accolades heaped on me by my fellows, it didn't make it any easier for me not having a playing contract.

There was much indecision and insecurity within the football club and I recall speaking with Don Revie and seeking his advice. He had played for England and had been a top class professional footballer for most of his adult life. He hadn't been overly friendly with me since I arrived, but I knew some of the other players greatly respected him. I believed, because of the respect people at the club, I don't mean just players, but the directors had for him too, my own thoughts were that if anyone knew what I should do, it would be Don Revie.

When I approached him and asked for a few moments of his time, he was dismissive of me and told me to make it quick because he was busy and had to be somewhere else. I told him of my concerns at Leeds, and hurriedly asked him if he thought I should contact other football clubs and try to get myself sorted elsewhere away from the football club.

He was clearly put out by my comment and became indignant with me. He looked at me full in the face and asked if I really wanted to play for Leeds United, if my heart was playing for Leeds United? I told him it was and I would do anything to sign professional terms for the club. 'Well, then, wait until the new manager comes in then see what happens.'

He walked away without uttering a further word on the matter. I felt very foolish when it was revealed a couple of days later that Don Revie was the new manager of the football club! I remember, at the time this happened there was a popular song doing the rounds, it was an Everly Brothers number called *Walk Right Back*. When I learned that Don Revie had been made Leeds manager I believed my time at the club was over, and the song seemed appropriate to my circumstances. In the back of my mind I was preparing myself for the *Walk Right Back* to Johannesburg.

At the club there seemed to be mixed feelings among the players about the appointment, many saw it as a good choice, others believed it not to be. I was undecided, my only dealings with him had left me feeling very much like an outsider. He hadn't been as warm or welcoming as many of the other players, this left me feeling uncomfortable when in his presence or company.

I have to be honest when I say, I don't think he liked me as a person back then, or when he passed away in 1989, simply because I didn't conform. He often referred to me as being a difficult person, and something of a square peg in a round hole. I never understood what this meant, but I believe he was referring to me being different in every way to many of those who were not ashamed to display an openly sycophantic manner and attitude towards him.

I preferred to keep myself to myself and maintain my own counsel where he was concerned, mainly because I respected that he was my manager, not my friend, and in his position he yielded the power and influence over my career and therefore my future life lay in his hands.

I carried on training and working hard to impress everyone at the club, I did not deviate from my routines, many miles of cross country running, always alone, and as part of the structured training, weights and using a medicine ball to build up my body strength. I achieved as much work with a football as I could manage. A week or so passed and Mr Revie, or 'boss' as he told everyone at the club he wanted to be called, never spoke a word to me or even glanced at me. I felt anonymous, which is almost as bad as being singled out for being a different colour.

He had all but dismissed my presence when he was a player, one of the reasons behind that was because I was on trial. Now he was the player-manager, I was sure that if he was interested in signing me he would have to be more communicative. He wasn't, and I felt ostracised. He would ask Les Cocker to get me to do additional training work on my own, practising crossing and shooting. They even had me trying to cross a ball into a dustbin from many yards away. I didn't know why I was being targeted for such treatment, the lowest point came when he had me sweeping the terracing.

I did everything that was asked of me, not only out of personal pride but because I wanted to play for Leeds United. As far as I was concerned, this was the only club I could ever and would ever play professional football for in England. I desperately wanted to be part of their future.

Then, totally out of the blue, Syd Owen came to the house at Noster Hill and asked to speak with me. He said the boss wanted to see me urgently, and to make my way to the ground. That was all he said, there was no intimation of anything good or bad, he gave me no idea or suggestion what it was about.

Inside, I knew it was decision time. It was a worrying walk I made down to the ground that afternoon. I began planning my options, I hadn't much in the way of belongings to pack should I have to leave for South Africa, so I could be out of the house within a couple of hours if necessary. To be honest, it was all negative thoughts I had, as I made way to the stadium. I reflected upon how the boss and I had not been friends prior to him becoming manager, nor had we made any effort to mix or socialise. He always seemed to keep me at arm's length, I was sure that there was no way he would offer me a contract!

I was close to tears when I walked into his office, he was

stood beside his desk, looking morose and deadly serious.

'Albert, how do you think you have done in your three months here?' he asked. I assured him I had always given my best in training and in games, and as a person representing the club in the city. I told him I loved the club and desperately wanted to stay.

'I have had some contradictory reports about you, and they concern me. Some people say you glide past players with ease and you can do almost anything with a football. Others tell me that you don't like getting stuck in when it matters. I've been watching you in training and in your extra work with Les, sometimes you amaze me, your skill and pace is breathtaking, your balance is majestic and the way you can leave players like Billy Bremner in your wake is bewildering. Everyone I speak to tells me you are a very nice man. I don't like you being a nice and polite man, I need you to toughen up Albert, don't be afraid to get stuck in where it hurts, don't give up the ball easily, fight for it, shout for it when you don't have it. What's your feelings on that? How do you feel, can you do that for me?'

I nodded my approval and told him I could and would, I sensed it wasn't good news but it wasn't bad, I expected him to tell me to keep working and training hard. I couldn't have been more wrong.

'Right then Albert Louis Johanneson, I want you here as part of my Leeds United. You have got yourself a contract, it's of extreme importance for both you and me at this moment, because I'm making you my first signing for this football club. I want to see passion in your game, the grit and determination side of your game has to be in there, let it emerge, I want you to fight for the cause of Leeds United, I want you to be give everything and if necessary, be prepared to die for the sake of this football club's success. I would do that, so I expect you to do it too. Don't let me down Albert, if you do, you'll be on the first plane back to South Africa. I'm taking a huge gamble on you delivering, so welcome to Leeds United, this is my Leeds United and you'll answer to me only do you understand that? Well done lad, now stop snivelling and get yourself back up the hill.'

I couldn't help myself, I had burst into tears and was sobbing hysterically. I must have thanked the boss one hundred times for giving me this opportunity. It got so bad that he threw a handkerchief at me and told me to sort myself out. He said he would get the club to draw up a contract and I would formally be asked to sign it when it was ready.

'First thing Albert, make sure you get yourself a decent shirt and suit and a tie. You're a professional footballer now, that's got a bit of status over here with our people, so pull yourself together and start acting like a man and not the shoeshine boy you think you are. People will look up to you Albert, so act accordingly, no more hiding in the shadows, get out there and enjoy your life and your time in Leeds.'

'Yes, boss,' I barked back at him, 'I'll do all of that, I'll go get some new clothes now.'

Leaving the ground I had the broadest, proudest smile on my face, I had done it, I had achieved what I set out to do, I had got myself a professional contract in English football. It had taken three months, but that felt like a lifetime and now I was back to being on my own again, there was no one to celebrate with. I wanted to see my family and be with them to share the moment with me. It felt wonderful to know I had proved myself capable and able, yet the moment was tinged with sadness because I was alone.

As I walked back up towards Noster Hill I visited St Mary's church and thanked the Lord for taking care of me and in helping me succeed. It was as though a weight had been lifted from my shoulders, now I could settle down and try to make real roots in the city of Leeds.

I spoke with the minister at the church and told him the good news, I wanted to tell the world what I had achieved. He was thrilled and hugged me, but told me to be mindful that legally, nothing was concrete until a contract had been signed by all parties. Once that was done, then I truly could celebrate. He was right, but that didn't stop me feeling very happy and pleased with myself.

As soon as I got home, I wrote several letters to my family and friends in South Africa. As I completed each one, I felt emotional sadness well up inside and I cried. I loved what I had achieved but I missed my family and my life with them. It's something I have learned in my life, a family is the most important part of everyday life, without a family, a life isn't fulfilled.

# 5

# Not Quite a Whole New World

It was Wednesday, 5th April 1961 when the formal contract was signed and agreed by both Leeds United and Albert Johanneson. The signing was very much a low key affair, mainly because no one bothered too much about what was happening at Leeds United. Albert joined Leeds on the princely sum of roughly £15 a week.

In the 1960s, Leeds was very much a working class city. Sporting wise, it was a city more synonymous with rugby league. The first ever clubs were formed in the city in the 19th century and in 1952 Wales rugby union star, Lewis Jones, made the jump from union to league and signed for Leeds for a startling £6,000. He went on to be a rugby league hero in the city where he was better known as 'Golden Boy.'

The rugby team of that era had a reasonably consistent record of achievement. Having first won the Yorkshire Cup in 1922, they had gone on to win the Rugby League Challenge Cup on seven occasions, the most recent being in 1957 when they beat Barrow 9–7 at Wembley Stadium. At the end of the 1960–1961 season, they were crowned for the first time in the club's history, as Rugby League Champions.

Up to the time of Albert signing for the club, Leeds United had a somewhat chequered past and history. Originally formed in 1919 after Leeds City football club had been suspended and expelled from the football league for 'alleged' illegal payments to players, the new club had achieved very little in the way of inspiring the people of Leeds to follow the club with the round ball as opposed, to the oval one.

In 1923–1924 they were crowned as second division champions but were relegated back into the second tier just three years later having consistently struggled to attain a higher final league position of 18th. They dropped down in 1927 winning just 11 games all season and finishing second from bottom of the first division.

Prior to the 1960s, the greatest name associated with Leeds United had been a giant of a Welshman called John Charles. He remains one of the greatest players ever to represent the club and, it could be argued that it was he who first put Leeds United on the Yorkshire football map, because it was Charles' stylish performances that aroused greater public interest in what was happening at Elland Road.

Generally speaking, Leeds United was something of a yo-yo club between the first and second divisions. The season prior to Albert's arrival, they had again suffered relegation from the first division, and for a time in 1961, looked liable to drop down even further, this time into the third division north. A desperate run of results from 18 February to 3 April 1961 saw the club lose seven games, draw one and win one. The form was dire and club morale low. The situation undoubtedly hastened the departure of then manager, Jack Taylor who opted to resign as opposed to being sacked.

The appointment of a new manager from within may have been a cheap option, and no one ever categorically stated that they knew it was the right decision; it was always going to be a calculated risk. The club's finances were poor and the board of directors were forced into something of a reshuffle, with Sam Bolton standing down as chairman, and director Harry Reynolds, taking over.

Revie told the author in an interview in the 1970s that he hadn't simply accepted the job because it was there for him:

I couldn't ever be described as a 'yes man'. I had my own definite thoughts on how a football club should be run, on how its playing staff should be treated, and how in turn, they should treat others. I explained to the directors what I wanted to achieve and how I wanted to get there, the journey I wanted to lead the club through.

I had a plan. As a club and a team, before I took over as manager, we were a shambles. There were players who needed moving on, not necessarily because they were poor, but because they needed a fresh challenge. Jack Taylor couldn't identify that, and if he did, he never did anything to alter it. If he had remained in charge at the club, we would have been relegated, no two ways about it.

The one thing Jack had in place was an excellent scouting network across the world. I wanted to keep those contacts open and available to me and the club. There were some good available footballers playing the game in places like South Africa that were every bit as good as, if not better, than many in England or Europe.

At one time I fancied bringing in a new goalkeeper called Arthur Lightening. He had been at Forest, Coventry and Middlesbrough. He had what it takes to be a good goalkeeper, but he ran away when the going got tough for him over here. His confidence dipped and his form fell away. He ended up conceding dozens of goals in a short space of time and returned to South Africa. I considered trying to get him back and spoke to Raich Carter. He told me to steer clear because he had suffered the wrath of the fans and they had effectively broken him.

Raich was sad that he hadn't spotted the break in the player's confidence before it took hold, and felt some responsibility. I told him that it was down to the player's resolve in such situations and he shouldn't take responsibility for that. If a player isn't mentally and physically strong enough, then no matter how much support you give, he will struggle to achieve. I wanted a team of winners, so Arthur Lightening wasn't one I pursued. Despite that, I knew full well, that there were some decent players overseas and in particular, in South Africa.

Revie used his skills and influence at international level to learn as much as he could about the state and style of the game in South Africa. It wasn't a priority, but he knew with the financial restraints he had at Leeds that he would have to search far and wide to find quality to help his team challenge.

It needed a complete change to the mindset. Leeds United was viewed in the city and in football as a dreary unexciting team whose only ambition was to survive in the shadows of a rugby league club. I was determined to change that, but to do it properly the whole club needed to change. Harry Reynolds shared my vision and so I began to dismantle the past and create new, more positive history.

I saw in Albert Johanneson a bright talent that I could develop. He was quick, exciting and different in every way, and other players were enthused by his potential. He was a player I couldn't let go, he was already creating attention elsewhere with other clubs monitoring his situation and I saw it as a test of my own ambition and intentions.

Albert didn't know it, but two first division teams were watching his situation very closely, if I had allowed him to leave us, he would have been snapped up by someone else in a higher division. Had he known of the interest then he may well have spoken to those clubs and been offered far better terms. I know he would have gone and we would have lost out. That speaks volumes for his ability, but also about my desire not to lose out on anything. I was a winner with a winning attitude, I wanted winners at my club. Albert was my first signing for Leeds United, I had doubts about him, and to be truthful, it was Les Cocker who finally persuaded me that Albert was of sufficient quality to represent the club. Les said that Albert would light up every football pitch in Europe with his blistering pace and ball control. In signing him I was helping my own reputation as a manager with real vision, and a new, international image for the football club.

Don Revie was correct. Albert was totally unaware that he possessed football talent that was coveted elsewhere and had no idea that Wolverhampton Wanderers and Fulham had shown interest in taking him on trial, as well as Leeds. Certainly, he never mentioned it in our conversations or discussions and was surprised when I told him of this detail.

> I didn't know of their interest, it wouldn't have made any difference to me, I had come over for a trial with Leeds. It was Leeds I had committed myself to, the only reason I would have left would have been if Leeds had rejected me or ended their interest. Other than Germiston, Leeds was the only other place in the world that I physically regarded as a home.

Some years later, in 1999, I spoke with a gentleman who described himself as a South African football spotter, whose name I only knew as 'Malachai.' He explained to me that Albert's footballing talent was something that other English clubs were well aware of.

> Albert was very quiet, an unassuming sort of boy, he was the type of boy who you would never take any notice of. He was a bit like a chameleon, he adapted to each relevant situation, it was conditioned in him throughout his young

life growing up in the township. He had to adapt. That is, until he had got a ball at his feet. I've never seen anyone with such footballing skill, he was blessed with a real gift.

There were many people coming to watch him play in games around Johannesburg, scouts from other countries in Europe, like France and Holland would ask about him. I knew Barney Gaffney had links in England and he had moved quickly to get Albert sorted with a club, and a trial at Leeds United. What most people don't know, and I doubt Albert did either, is that if he (Albert) had waited a few more weeks he would have gone on trial elsewhere and may never have joined Leeds United.

Wolverhampton Wanderers were a successful club and they were very interested. They had visited the country and played football here, they knew the people here, they had been to watch Albert four or five times and were expected to come back to sort something out. It was a bit of a surprise when Albert joined Leeds. I tried to make the scouts at Wolverhampton aware, but they didn't move swiftly enough.

I know it sounds bad, but I lost money, commission money through Albert going to Leeds. I was upset by it and for a time I was bitter that Gaffney had moved in and had almost stolen Albert from my own backyard, it still hurts me today that I missed out on the greatest South African footballer of many generations, Albert Johanneson.

Back in Leeds, Albert was celebrating becoming a professional footballer, not in the manner in which his life has been previously portrayed, through alcohol, but by visiting the church and privately, through prayer, thanking all those people who had stood beside him in his early days in Leeds and elsewhere.

I was thrilled and things really changed for me. Overnight I had become accepted as part of a unit, the players shook my hand and told me how happy they were. I was one of them and part of the club. I had to ask myself why there was such a positive change in people's attitude towards me. I was bemused by the difference a signed piece of paper could make to my life. Albert Johanneson had become a somebody in England. It was as though it gave me an identity and I was very pleased about that.

I knew that personally none of these people appreciated who I really was, where I came from and what made me into the person I was and still am. I always felt that because I was black, I was viewed differently and treated differently.

Some of my playing colleagues would animatedly shout their way through conversations with me, as though they were speaking a different language and I had hearing problems. To be honest, I speak quietly and I like to think I can make my point without shouting or raising my voice, so I could easily have taken their actions as an insult. Putting it simply, they didn't know any better and it was them who didn't understand the situation.

I think because I was black, many white people saw me as having some sort of disability and inferiority. The vast majority of players and people at the football club were good people and I was generally happy to be one of their groups, yet, others made it clear that they didn't want to associate with me beyond football. I respected that choice and thankfully most of them moved on to other teams.

One of the biggest cultural challenges I encountered, was when Syd Owen pulled me to one side and told me the protocols of looking after the young apprentice who had been nominated to clean my boots and training plimsolls. I was mortified when I was told this. I didn't need anyone to look after my boots or kit, I could do that myself, it wasn't a task for a youth of any colour.

I asked Syd Owen if it would be deemed proper for a white apprentice to clean a black man's boots. He laughed, patted me on my shoulder and told me not to worry about such matters, assuring me it was nonsense. I always made sure my boots were reasonably clean before replacing them in the boot room so that I maintained protocol and didn't upset other colleagues.

I'm certain I should have been proud to have progressed to the stage where I had an apprentice looking after my kit, but I felt it was demeaning for any person to have to be subservient to another. For me, it was just a bit too much to take in so quickly, I was black, and not used to telling anyone, let alone a white person, what to do.

\* \* \* \* \*

Friday, 7th April 1961, was no different from any other day. For Albert, as usual, he had risen early and walked down to the Elland Road football ground for training.

It was raining heavily, and in the back of my mind I was planning my weekend around playing for the second team and then to maybe go out into the city and do a bit of dancing. Sunday morning would be spent at church and then relaxing and writing some more letters home.

Training felt a bit different that day, I thought I was imagining it, but it appeared that I was being worked much harder by Les Cocker and Syd Owen throughout the whole session. They were pushing balls ahead of me to run onto, and cross. It was non stop and the balls came at me from the right, the left and across the pitch. They were bouncing, fired hard, softly and some even needed to be headed to get them under control.

All the time I could see and hear Mr Revie somewhere in the background, yelling at me to control the ball much quicker and to push it on in one sweeping movement. Many of the balls were being launched way ahead of me and I couldn't get to them before they ran off the playing area. The boss was really vocal and having a go at me, I remember him losing his temper and screaming out: 'Fucking hell Albert lad, have you got lead in your boots? Run lad, run, don't just stand there waiting for the ball to come to you, get after it and get it into that bloody penalty area.'

I was exhausted and I think some of the other players, particularly those waiting for the crosses to come into the penalty area could see I was struggling. Jack Charlton kept telling me to keep running and to chase everything.

'Don't give up Albert, if you put the ball in the air and it comes into the penalty box, I'll win it with my head and put it into the bloody net, don't worry about that Albert, just get it in there for me,' he instructed.

I did as he asked and sure enough, Jack was soon heading the ball into the net. It felt good to have got something so right and made me believe that the trainers and manager knew what was best for my game.

At the end of training, as was my way, I remained on the training pitch and continued to train with the ball, crossing and dropping it into the centre of the penalty area. After about half an hour or so, Les Cocker came out and told me I had to stop training for the day, and to get in the bath and changed.

'We've worked you hard today Albert, how do you feel after that? You did alright though, I'm pleased you are still working hard, it reflects well on you. Now get yourself off home and changed, and this evening, put your feet up and relax.'

The changing room was empty when I got there and I quickly bathed and changed. As was the procedure, I checked the team sheet for the second team on my way out, anticipating on seeing my name listed there. I had to do a double take when it wasn't there. I felt my stomach knot up and an air of sadness crept over me.

In the very week I had signed a player's contract I had been dropped from the second string. I remembered the words spoken by Grenville Hair three months earlier: 'Albert, things will happen in football that really surprise you, nothing is straight forward, it's a tough world and only the best survive, especially at good clubs like this. It's character building and every time you get knocked back, you need to learn from it and come back even stronger.'

I tried to put the exclusion out of my mind and made my way back to Noster Hill and sat down to eat my lunch. There was a telephone call to the house and Mrs Wineley excitedly told me it was a call for me. I put on a brave face trying to hide the disappointment I felt about being dropped and took the receiver from her 'Albert, it's Les Cocker here, are you okay? I'm just calling to wish you the best of luck for tomorrow's game, I may not get chance tomorrow so go out and enjoy it.'

I was surprised that he had bothered to call and that he was wishing me luck. I replied, 'What do you mean, sir? You have made a mistake. I'm not playing tomorrow, I checked the second team, team sheet, my name did not appear on it.'

'Albert, I haven't made a mistake, and you are right, your name doesn't appear on the second team, team sheet, there's a very good reason for that, it's because you're playing in the first eleven against Swansea tomorrow. It's your football league debut Albert, you've earned it. Now eat your lunch and get yourself relaxed and in a positive frame of mind.'

I was shaking with excitement, I became nervous and could hardly hold the cutlery to eat my lunch. Mrs Wineley was thrilled and gave me a huge hug, she was crying for me. 'I'm proud of you Albert, well done' she told me.

This was it, my big moment, representing Leeds United in a football league second division fixture at Elland Road against Swansea Town. I wondered what sort of team Swansea might be, and what kind of football they might play. It was all a bit of a blur, everything seemed to happen so quickly and before I knew it, it was match day and I was walking through the players' area of Elland Road.

For an all too brief moment, I felt like an equal, I forgot that I was viewed differently by fellow footballers. I was walking along a narrow corridor to the changing rooms and heard someone from the Swansea dressing room area deliberately shout out in my hearing, 'They have got a black bastard playing for them, or is he just the boot boy?'

I felt my heart skip a beat and suddenly my stomach was twitching with nerves. All my insecurities returned and flowed through my mind, I felt unworthy and not a little concerned by the comment. Part of me wanted to go back to the room and put the loudmouth right, but I wasn't sure that such action might cause a riot and therefore trouble for me. Instead, I let it go and said nothing.

Billy Bremner and Freddie Goodwin were my rocks that day. Before the kick off they led me out of the playing tunnel and out onto the pitch, this was so I could acclimatise and feel the atmosphere as the stadium began to fill up. It was a very different feeling, sensing that from the pitch.

Freddie told me that it was going to be tough for me being a left winger, playing next to the stands and the crowd. He told me to stay focused on the ball and to watch and listen to the game and the Leeds players, and not to the crowd. 'You'll hear the crowd Albert, every last one of them especially the visiting bastards, they'll crucify you if you let them. Away crowds are not the kindest, so it's best to try and switch off, and remember, it's not about you at all, it's all about Leeds United. They hate every one of us, not just you. In two hours time they will be leaving this great place and returning to their shit hole grounds, then you'll be nothing but a memory, so my advice is to give them something to remember you by, bad memories. Rip their team apart, the football is your voice, make everything you do count.'

Billy looked on and was laughing, he told me to take a good look at both wings, especially where I would be playing because there were divots and sods missing that could affect the roll of the ball. I told him I would check everything out.

I was so busy concentrating on the playing surface that I eventually wandered off from the main group of players and ended up on my own. I looked up to see and hear a small group of people, Swansea supporters stood on the terracing calling me names. They were jumping up and down, mimicking monkeys and calling me darkie. I ignored them, put my head down and walked back towards the main group of Leeds players. My body language must have looked weak and extremely negative.

The next thing I knew was Billy Bremner rushing past me. He was walking in a 'determined manner' towards the vocal group stood on the terracing. He stopped short of the side of the pitch, confronted them and asked what the problem was. They began to laugh at him, calling him a 'pygmy Jock' and a 'carrot head.' I heard one of them call him a 'Scots bastard' to which Billy gave them one of his off the cuff comments that still makes me laugh now. 'Well boys, you've got me summed up, but not him. He's black because it's his natural skin colour and he comes from South Africa. You're black because you live in a filthy mining town and you don't wash, you filthy bastards. There, how do you like it when people say things to you and call you names that are offensive and untrue? It's bad, isn't it? It's wrong and you know it, now grow up and shut up, you are here to watch football, not hurt people.'

A number of other players had walked over to give Billy some support and back up. The group on the terracing either realised that Billy was speaking sense, or they felt intimidated. I'm not certain, but whatever it was, it had the desired effect and they retreated back up the steps and walked away without further comment.

Billy came to me and told me to use the contempt I must surely feel for being treated like that positively, and allow that emotion to build up inside, control it, and release it into my game. That way I would arouse passion and show desire to prove to my detractors how wrong they were. Like Freddie Goodwin, he told me the best way to punish them was with my skill.

In a few moments I heard more comments of 'nigger' and 'darkie' coming from elsewhere on the terraces. It felt as though it was coming from all four sides of the ground, so I left the pitch and returned to the changing rooms. I went to the toilet and locked myself inside, creating for myself a bit of space and time to get my thoughts and actions together.

The problem was, I didn't feel animosity to those calling me names, I think I had become a little hardened to some of the name calling, mainly because of the way I was spoken to in South Africa and, also because I didn't know or care about the football supporters of Swansea or what they thought of me. So I couldn't really get upset and angry as Billy suggested. I was feeling more nervous about how my performance on the pitch would be gauged by my colleagues and the Leeds management. I wanted to show them they had made the right decision and was desperate to put in a good game.

By the time we came out onto the pitch for kick-off, I could hear the crowd chanting songs and the smell of cigarette smoke, damp and sweat seemed to be everywhere. I ran out and began to warm up with the rest of the team, short sprints, stretches, generally trying to evaporate my nervous tension. The abusive calls from the terraces were incessant and quite varied: 'Blackie come and clean my boots,' 'There's a nig-nog playing, 'Look at the little sambo.'

It's hard to describe how I felt knowing that many of the people in that stadium didn't like me and apparently wanted me to fail. Some seemed desperate for me to make my first error so that it could be magnified and their criticism could unsettle me. I knew that everything I did would have to be perfect if I was to quieten the abusers, I knew that I had to find some emotion and put passion into my game, and with less than five minutes to kick-off, there I was pontificating about my mental and emotional strength.

As I looked towards the Swansea football team, I saw a few of them gathered and pointing towards me. They were laughing at me and I heard one of them say, 'Bloody hell, Leeds must be desperate, they have got a darkie playing for them.' It was just what I needed, I trotted up to the halfway line, I was wide on the wing and looked directly at them. They mouthed a few further obscenities and I responded by laughing at them and shaking my head in pathetic disbelief.

Billy came running over to me and asked if I was okay and ready to do battle. He had such a way with words, he wasn't eloquent, but he put passion into everything he said, especially on the pitch. I remember exactly what it was he said to me shortly before the kick-off against Swansea. 'Albert, are you ready for this? Are you ready to put this bunch in their place? I fucking hate these Swansea bastards, more so now for the way they are treating you, let's tear at them with good football and make them shut their big stupid mouths.' He grabbed hold of my arms and was looking directly into my eyes. 'Let's do it Albert, let's bloody do it.'

I felt passion, I felt inspired and ready to follow Billy into battle, he was a true leader.

Just before we kicked off, a few of the team came over to me and gave me various 'pats' on my back and wished me good luck. Allan Humphreys, our goalkeeper that day, came rushing out to remind me to keep looking for space on the wing as he would be clearing balls for me to run onto. He was a decent enough man, but as a goalkeeper I never really had the greatest confidence in him. I felt he lacked the command of his penalty area and although I hadn't played in the first team before, I had watched him play in competitive games and knew his areas of weakness. In my opinion he cost Leeds a goal in many of the games I saw, yet as a reflex goalkeeper, he was more than capable of making great saves.

Our team that day consisted of: Humphreys, Hair, Kilford, Smith, Goodwin, McConnell, Fitzgerald, Bremner, Charlton, Cameron, Johanneson. When the referee blew his whistle to signal kick-off, I felt an immense pride inside and for a few seconds my thoughts were with my family and all the people I grew up with, people who had supported me back in the township.

All the time behind me on the terraces I could hear

monkey chants and the name calling got progressively worse. It seemed a while before I got involved in the game, I was running up and down and around the pitch trying to make space and take a pass, but it wasn't happening. I was getting really frustrated at not being able to shake off my markers, a fact that was noticed by some of the spectators who accused me of hiding.

I reacted to one call and tried to explain to the man in the crowd that I was trying to get involved, all that achieved was even more abuse and a whole section of the crowd telling me to concentrate on the game.

Then I took a pass from Freddie Goodwin. I remember hearing the Leeds crowd roar with anticipation and feeling the pounding of footsteps approaching from behind. I knew by the pace of the footsteps that it had to be a Swansea player intent on recovering the ball. I swivelled and turned left then quickly to my right. The Swansea player launched himself at me. It was a lunge that wasn't meant to win the ball, but hurt me. The training sessions with Billy Bremner had taught me how to avoid such thuggish behaviour. I sidestepped the player who went flying into the muddy turf, the uncomfortable landing caused him some pain and much more embarrassment, as he called out to me, 'You black twat, I'll break your neck for this.'

Then, it was as though time stood still, I glanced up and saw another Swansea player rushing towards me, his eyes were focused on me and not the ball. Behind him, I saw a huge gap on the wing. I waited until he had committed himself to the tackle and rolled the ball past him, skipping beyond his flying torso and outstretched arms.

At last I was running into space, tearing up the wing and feeling absolutely wonderful. I felt like a wild animal unleashed from a cage. I could hear the roar of encouragement from the crowd. I cut inside another Swansea player and crossed the ball into the penalty area. It was cleared and the attack came to nothing, but the confidence that run provided to me and to the crowd was immeasurable. They had seen some of what I was capable of and seemingly liked it.

I could sense that my colleagues were confident that I could deliver for them and I gradually became more involved in the game, all the time looking for space to receive the ball and attack Swansea. For a time it seemed as though I was the one Leeds player everyone wanted the ball passed to, I was creating opportunities and suddenly, Swansea had two men closely marking my every move. They weren't as nimble as I was, they were big brutes, strong but slow.

Up front for Leeds, Jack Charlton was playing at centre forward and winning everything in the air. He constantly reminded me to keep launching the ball into the Swansea box and assuring me that he would get onto the end of most of my crosses.

Everything I did seemed to come off that day, the Swansea players were rash and leaping into challenges with me. They seemed desperate to be the first to knock me off my feet and win the validation of their colleagues. I was having none of it, I skipped, hopped and jumped around each of them, avoiding virtually every challenge and leaving them on their backsides as I ran off with the ball. This seemed to make them all the more bitter and angry towards me.

It was only a matter of time, but eventually one player did clatter into me and landed on top of me after he literally kicked my feet away in a wrestling type tackle. As he lay on top of me he pinched my leg with his fingers and thumb and snarled into my face, 'Nigger, take the piss out of me again and I will kick your fucking arse all the way back to South Africa.'

I pushed him off and told him to get away from me as his breath smelt heavily of alcohol. The referee was there and heard his comment to me. He asked if I was okay, so I told him what had just happened and what had been said. I was surprised when he laughed and told me that I would have to get used to it. 'You are black, you are different, I promise you'll take a lot more of that before your career here is finished. My advice is don't listen to it, don't get involved in their antics, if it happens again, tell him to fuck off, it's only words and words won't kill you.'

Although it shocked me, it was as good a piece of advice as I ever received in my time in football. When I saw him after the game I thanked him for saying what he had, it really helped me. He congratulated me on a fine performance and said he thought I would be a star in English football with my skills. It felt very good to hear such nice compliments.

I took so many kicks and knocks during that game that I began to feel physically drained, it seemed that each time I got the ball, part of the crowd yelled abuse.

On the pitch the opposition didn't like it either and desperately tried to hurt me and stop me from playing and enjoying my game. Despite that, I was thriving with my freedom on the wing and being released on countless runs towards the Swansea goal.

I crossed several balls for Jack, but each time the keeper seemed to save it or Jack's header missed the target. On one run, I ghosted past several Swansea players and for a moment, selfishly thought about continuing my run towards the Swansea goal. Then I looked up and saw him racing into the penalty area, I dropped the ball directly into his path, onto his head and he did the rest, smacking it in the Swansea net.

I didn't know what to do, I was reluctant to celebrate in front of all the white men in the crowd, I was worried it may cause a riot so stood still and looked on. I felt numb and closed my eyes to thank God for helping me. To my amazement, when I looked up, Jack and several other Leeds players were sprinting towards me with their arms held wide open. They grabbed hold of me and embraced me. I was emotionally lost, all I could hear among the shouting players were the words, 'What a fucking ball, what a fucking ball, Albert, Albert, what a fucking cross. Goal, goal, goal.'

It is a moment I will never ever forget, my colleagues were pleased with me and impressed, they were thanking me for my effort in getting the goal. I wanted to cry with happiness, instead, all I could say was thank you, thank you, thank you. I felt like I was sitting on top of the world and although I hadn't scored the goal myself I realised how important my role had been in Jack scoring.

Jack ran back alongside me and said to me, 'Albert, you are a fucking star pal. Me and you, we are going to murder defences in this league, just keep doing what you are doing and we'll get plenty of chances for more goals, we are going to be a real good team with you playing out wide.'

It was our defence that let us down in that game, Swansea weren't brilliant at all, but they were organised and strong, and put us under a bit of pressure. Looking on I could see that our defence lacked pace, and we were caught out by many balls that weren't properly cleared.

I felt rather sorry for Allan Humphrey, our goalkeeper, who seemed to be struggling to be heard and I'm not certain that it was his fault. The problem was the defence wasn't confident and so tended to be disorganised when put under pressure.

Individuals weren't prepared to take responsibility and so we lacked leadership in many parts of our rear ranks. Full back, John Kilford, seemed to be out of sorts, he was one of a number of players who I felt didn't really seem to fit into the Don Revie game plan.

Jack Charlton and Billy Bremner were strong and loud, vocal in their support and constantly searching for the ball. Jack was great throughout my debut, he never stopped making runs and dragged the Swansea full backs and half backs all over the place, giving me more space to run at them with the ball at my feet.

The final score was a 2–2 draw, I was disappointed because it was a game I thought we deserved to win and had our defence been quicker to respond and read the game, we would have won.

Afterwards, the boss said he was satisfied with our performance, he pointed out that silly mistakes had cost us goals and that we would have to work hard to remedy that in future games.

For me, I felt pleased with my game and knew I hadn't let anyone down. I knew that I had won some of the Leeds fans over because the more I took players on, the more enthusiastic and vocal they became. I felt them willing me on. As I sat on the bench in the changing room, I came over all emotional, and had to cover my face with my hands as I had a discreet cry; a football team changing room is not a place where you can hide. The players noticed my tears and gathered round to show their support, everyone seemed to want to tell me how well I had done.

The communal bath had been filling with hot water and the changing room was full of steam. I waited while the rest of the players stripped off and jumped into the water. Billy Bremner was puffing away on a cigarette and asked me why I wasn't getting in the bath. He advised me to get my boots off, 'Are you shy Albert?' he asked.

I said I didn't think the other players would want to share a bath with a black man.

'What are you talking about man, why is that Albert? What have you got that makes you different from us? Get your bloody strip off and get in there.'

I didn't have time to respond. Some of the players surrounded me, took hold of me and with a great cheer threw me into the bath. I was shaking with excitement, I felt so happy and content. A few minutes earlier, the football supporters and players of Swansea had made me feel very different: hated. Now I felt I was amongst my own kind of people, they were all white, and they couldn't see, or at least didn't show, that they saw me as black and different.

The insecurity of feeling different was something I would have to work at. Without any doubt, it was a social stigma being black in an all white domain. Yet some of my colleagues went out of their way constantly to reassure me that we were all one big family. That was all very nice in the safety of the team changing room, but the reality outside of that, beyond Elland Road stadium, was very different. I clearly wasn't able to be in the company of the players all the time, and away from the playing side of life, I suffered greatly.

After the game with Swansea, we left the stadium, and again, I was immediately targeted for racist comments and abuse by some Swansea fans who remained in the area of the ground. Again it was Billy Bremner who sorted these people out. It was dark in the car park and I felt vulnerable and uncomfortable, so hid behind some of the other players who had formed a human shield around me.

As Billy made to move towards the group and express his opinion of their poor attitude, they scattered, like terrified birds hearing the nearby sound of a shotgun, disappearing into the night without shouting another word towards me. I waited in the main car park behind the West Stand for a time, talking to other players and was introduced to their families. Each time I was asked the same question by their respective partners: 'Are you married? Do you have a girlfriend in South Africa?'

I explained that I hadn't, again, the response was virtually identical, it went something on the lines of: 'Well, we will have try to find you someone, we need to get you a good woman, Albert.'

A relationship wasn't something I had considered since arriving in Leeds, because there seemed to be way too much animosity being shown towards me by various quarters of the city. In places it just didn't feel safe; some of the dance hall stories I had heard of did little to change my opinion.

I knew of one black person in Leeds who had been kicked unconscious by a group of white local people outside a dance hall, simply because he had supposedly looked at the girlfriend of one of the dancers in an 'enticing and encouraging' way. He ended up in hospital with a broken leg and fractured skull, and later, on his return home, had his house set on fire by a group intent on forcing him out of the area. They achieved their purpose, he left Leeds and moved to Bradford with his family.

# 6

# I'm Blessed

The day after making my Leeds United debut I went to church and thanked the Lord for blessing me with the skill and desire to achieve my goals. I found it difficult to stay focused on the church service, because I was still on an emotional high. My Leeds debut was at that point in my life, the greatest achievement I had made. I couldn't stop crying.

Some other members of the congregation noticed my tears and falsely believed that I was sad. After the service I was able to explain that I was overwhelmed because of my achievement on the football pitch the day previously. One or two people were able to understand my emotional outburst, others were dismissive of my joy and believed that I should not bring professional success into a religious environment because, in the eyes of God, we were all equals.

When I looked into the eyes of those people who questioned my religious integrity, I saw first hand, envy. I felt saddened that not everyone wanted to share my fleeting success with me. This was nothing to do with my skin colour or cultural differences; this was the fabled green eyed monster better known as jealousy. I had previously never witnessed anything like it. In the community where I came from, every black person wanted their neighbour to achieve and do well. They would go out of their way to make sure it happened; there was no back stabbing or deliberate comments that were meant to undermine, or negative statements that were damaging to a person's self confidence.

As I left church I was embraced by a few people who

had gathered outside, one older man took hold of my hand and thanked me for the performance I had given on the Elland Road pitch the day before. He told me I was to stay positive, he saw me as a brave man, blessed with skill and talent that not many footballers can lay claim to. I remember him stating that I had given the football public of Leeds, real hope for a good future. I was embarrassed and didn't know what to say. I told him I liked playing for Leeds and would always give of my best for them and the supporters. He hugged me and told me I had the manners of a white man.

Knowing what I did about the behaviour of certain white people, I wasn't certain whether to take that as an insult or a compliment, but accepted it as the latter and thanked him.

As I made the short walk home I was stopped by a man and his young son. 'Are you the blackie who played for us yesterday? You were amazing, can we have your autograph please?' I thanked him for what was clearly meant to be a positive comment and not as inoffensive a remark as it sounded and was pleased to sign my autograph.

As I continued on my way, life felt great, suddenly, people weren't being rude to me. They were saying good things about my football skills. The one void that still existed inside me was missing my family. I wished they could have been there to experience those incredible moments.

When I returned to the house, I was greeted by the beaming smile of Mrs Wineley. 'You've had a few telephone calls this morning Albert, people are keen to congratulate you and say well done on yesterday. The local newspaper wants to speak with you and some of the local kids have been round wanting to know if you would like to play football with them later today. I'd advise against that though love.'

On hearing this, once again my emotions got the better of me, and I cried. No matter how much reassurance

I received from people who cared, I just couldn't understand that this was all happening. It was like being in a permanent daze, I enjoyed the good attention and adulation but feared that as quickly as it arrived, it may all be taken away from me.

That afternoon I took a walk around Beeston and found a group of children kicking an old battered football around on a piece of wasteland. For a moment, I stood and watched. The game was brought to an abrupt halt when some of the children saw me and excitedly came running over to where I was stood. 'Albert, Albert, please come and play with us, show us some skill and tricks.'

I couldn't resist and whipped off my shoes and socks and took control of the ball with my bare feet. At first they laughed at the sight of me in bare feet, but I quickly silenced them as I juggled the ball and did a bit of showing off. I told them that I would come back each week and teach them the same skills and tricks.

I didn't realise it at the time, but I was beginning to set down roots within the community. Football clubs today (1990s) have football in the community schemes, yet looking back, it was something I was successfully doing in 1961.

The following week was all a bit of a whirlwind, training was thorough and 'the boss' really worked us hard, he was much more involved than Mr Taylor and took a personal interest in our training performances. My good friend Gerry Francis was back in training, he too was a winger, a right winger. He suffered a bit through injury and had been in and out of the first team since he first arrived and made a goalscoring debut against Everton in October 1959.

Many people told me that Gerry's debut was a special one. He had run Everton ragged and scored a sensational goal that had thrilled the entire ground and saw some of the Everton players later congratulate him. Gerry and I had many links, he was a black South African, from Johannesburg. Like so many of us from that city, he too had learned shoe repairing skills as a means of earning a living in that country. Barney Gaffney who had been something of a mentor to me knew Gerry. Because of these and the Leeds connection, we were to become good friends and it was a very proud moment for me when I acted as best man at Gerry and Anna's wedding in 1962.

That particular week in training both Gerry and I seemed to excel. We were motivating each other, running at players and past them, it was as though we had a psychological understanding and appreciation of each other's game. We clicked. The boss told me that he had seen nothing like the pair of us when we were in full flow and running at defenders. Gerry and I discussed the chances of us both playing in the same team for the following game, which was away at Stoke City. It would be special and unique in many ways, an English football first: two black South African footballers playing in the same team in a competitive league fixture. It would communicate a fantastic and positive message to countless black children across the world if it could happen.

A local journalist interviewed me and prompted the suggestion that it could happen. He asked how it would make me feel. I told him that it was a privilege to represent Leeds United no matter who I was playing alongside. If Gerry and I were in the same team it would be because we were good enough as footballers, and not for any other reason.

A couple of days before the Stoke City game, the boss called me into his office and asked me to sit down. I was worried and uncomfortable because I thought I had done something wrong and was about to be told I was being dropped or something.

'You are settling in well Albert, everyone has been impressed by the way you conduct yourself. I don't think I have seen anyone quicker than you when you set off down the wing, your crossing and ball delivery is exceptional. Having said that, I would like to see you being a bit more ruthless and greedy, instead of getting to the byline and crossing, get into the penalty area and try going for goal yourself. As you know, centre forwards aren't as quick as wingers and often take time to create and find the right goalscoring position inside the penalty area. I can see this may frustrate you, having to wait for your colleagues to catch up with you, so when that happens, just go for goal yourself. In training you are the same, don't be frightened to shoot, just let loose Albert, give the opposition goalkeeper and defenders something to worry about. Even if you are 25 yards out, if you think you can score, go for it. I'm playing you and Gerry on the wings this Saturday, I want you both to get at the full backs and get in behind them whenever you can, cross and shoot, whichever you feel is the best option. It's your choice Albert, we trust you to do the right thing.'

I was ecstatic, it was the greatest thing anyone had ever said about my game, the boss inspired me to do as he asked. I couldn't wait to tell Gerry the news that we were both in line to play at Stoke.

The following day, Les Cocker confirmed the news and told me to take it easy in training as the boss didn't want me getting hurt or injured. To be honest, now I had made it into the first team, I wasn't about to give that position up lightly. To keep it, I had to maintain my effort and desire to learn and develop, so taking it easy wasn't an option for me. That aside, I felt young and invincible, injuries were not something I considered or thought about.

We were given a briefing on the Stoke team, and the boss confused me a little, first he made them sound like world beaters, in the next sentence he reminded us that if we did everything he told and asked of us, then we would beat them.

As we arrived in Stoke I saw what I considered to be an unpleasant city, the football stadium itself was surrounded by tight narrow streets lined with terraced houses not dissimilar to Beeston, though it has to be said, Beeston had far more greenery and open spaces that provided fresh air to my lungs.

The city of Stoke I saw that day was an oppressive and dire sort of place, much worse than Leeds. Its people looked miserable, uninspired and depressed, almost as if they were lost souls aimlessly wandering the area. Today though, they had something new in their lives, they had two black footballers playing against their team, and we soon learned how upsetting that was for them.

I was stood outside the main entrance to the stadium, there were many people wandering about, some were wearing red and white scarves and hats denoting them as Stoke City supporters.

All of a sudden a man stood in front of me, he was smiling at me. I nodded and smiled back at him. I felt intimidated by his presence, so avoided my gaze towards the floor. 'What you doing here? Are you here to clean shoes or what?'

I said nothing in response and moved to walk away from him. He yanked me back grabbing hold of my arm and spinning me round so I faced him. I wanted to run but there was nowhere to run to. His face was contorted into a grimace as he shouted out, 'Look what we have here boys, a little negro, where's your spear Zulu man?'

I was so frightened that I was unable to speak or move. A well dressed man in a suit intervened and pushed me back inside the reception area, asking if I was the black man Johanneson from South Africa? I confirmed I was and he told me not to go outside on my own again, and to go to the Leeds dressing room without delay.

To this day I don't know who he was, but he had a certain air of authority about him that made me think he was one of the Stoke directors.

I was still shaking when I got to the Leeds dressing room, some of the players had gone out onto the pitch to have a look around. Hurriedly, I joined them in an attempt to get some air into my lungs and calm myself down.

The Stoke fans were an obscene foul-mouthed bunch, and there was a constant barrage of abuse hurled at me throughout the day. I wandered around the pitch with

Gerry Francis before we all returned to the changing room for the pre-match talk. I felt quietly satisfied and proud that Gerry and I were to play in the same side at this level. Privately, I prayed that we would both put in performances that showed our worth and ability.

Inside the changing room the boss was pacing up and down speaking to each player individually. He told me to do what I was best at, running at defenders. He would often describe opposition defences as being like carthorses, slow and cumbersome. He spoke of individual players, their skills and strengths and weaknesses. He told me that I could expect a 'good kicking' off the Stoke defenders because they were resolute in stopping teams from playing an attacking game.

Such comments made me wary of the damage that crude challenges could personally cause to me or my colleagues. There were a couple of changes to the team that played against Swansea, John McCole returned as centre forward and Jack Charlton reverted back to playing at centre half. Freddie Goodwin didn't feature.

I think Jack saw my nervousness, because before we left the changing room he told me not to think about how rough the opposition could be, but to concentrate on getting behind them and getting the ball into the penalty area.

The game itself was something of a non-event, less than memorable for me. It was a fiercely fought battle and not the style or type of football that helped my game. The pitch quickly turned into a field of mud, each time I got the ball it seemed to get stuck under my feet, allowing the Stoke defenders to get on top of me and clear their lines.

Centre forward, John McCole continually had words with me throughout the game. He wasn't happy that I could read the game and was aware of his positioning. I tried to explain to him that the state of the pitch was making it difficult for me to get past players. This resulted in my trying to get the ball to him almost as soon as I received it, many times he was out of position and unprepared to receive the pass. We both became frustrated with each other, resulting, at the final whistle, with him calling me 'useless.' That hurt me a great deal, it really knocked my confidence.

After the game, the dressing room atmosphere was flat. It was a game we all thought we could have won, instead, we had been dragged into a physical battle. It was a game where both Gerry Francis and I didn't perform as well as we could. The boss tried to lift our spirits, reminding us we hadn't conceded a goal and had rarely looked like doing so as we had resolutely defended our goal.

The fact that he didn't mention the attacking side of our game spoke volumes of his private opinion. I felt as though I should have done more, maybe I should have put in greater effort, albeit, I had nothing more I could give. It was as though I had let everyone down.

As we left the stadium, John McCole apologised for blaming me for his lack of efforts on the Stoke goal. He shook my hand and told me not to dwell on the performance or the result, it was gone and there was nothing we could do about it. Next up, a week later, was Lincoln City, at Elland Road. It was a game we had to win if we were to pull ourselves away from the relegation area of the second division. Lincoln were struggling at the bottom of the division and as the game was at Leeds, we would be expected to turn in a winning performance.

It was the following day when I learned that Gerry Francis, Leeds United and myself had made history the previous day. It was the first time two black footballers had played together in the same team in an English football league fixture. Whilst it wasn't all that significant back then, it certainly meant much more to Gerry and I than it did to the people of Britain. It was a milestone in the game, and one day, I hope other black footballers will celebrate it as a major milestone in not only worldwide equality, but as an incentive that no matter where we are raised, we can all achieve our dreams, be it through sport or in business.

I still recall, as the referee was about to blow his whistle to start the game at Stoke, looking across the field and seeing Gerry lining up on the opposite wing from me, looking every bit a professional footballer and not a random black person making up the numbers.

We were both there because we had earned it and, we were as good as, if not, in some cases, better than, several other footballers out there on the pitch. I genuinely believe that now, but back in 1961, I wasn't so confident in my own ability. My self-belief wasn't as confirmed as it is now, that comes with age and experience. Memories of what Gerry and I achieved that day still make me smile with pride, and although we didn't win, we still competed and played our part in earning the team a vital point.

Sadly, for that season at least, Gerry and I never featured again in the same Leeds line up for a league game.

\* \* \* \* \*

Initially, my Sundays and much of my time away from football were spent at church or resting up in my room. I had achieved one of my immediate aims in purchasing a transistor radio, and for many hours, I would lie on my bed and listen to the various dance sounds, occasionally getting off the bed and dancing around the floor in the privacy of my room. I even tried to sing like the great Elvis Presley whose song *Wooden Heart* was all over the radio at the time.

Some of the other players at Noster Hill would moan at my constant singing. Clive Middlemass was one in particular who didn't seem to appreciate my tones and would laughingly ask if I could whistle instead of sing as it sounded much better!

The following week I found myself out and about in the city much more than I had previously ever been. I spent some time exploring but most of it was socialising, visiting other black communities and trying to make roots and form friendships. There was a clear white, black divide in Leeds and across England.

One of the few white people who socialised with me more than most was Grenville Hair; he was very much a man who saw everyone as equals. Many of the social places we visited together, restaurants and public houses, welcomed Grenville with open arms, provided him with a complimentary meal and a free drink or two. I found it hard when I was treated like a second rate citizen and, despite Grenville getting his free, I would be told that I had to pay for my food or drink.

There was one cafeteria that would ask me to go through to the rear of the kitchen to eat. The owner, a man called Fred, told me that I would put people off coming in if I was sat in the eating area. He was genuinely being serious and I felt that what he said was true. Nevertheless, I was really offended by being made such an outcast. I eventually stopped visiting his premises.

Then one day I bumped into him in the market, I was a bit embarrassed when I saw him as I thought he was going to ask me why I didn't use his establishment. He looked sheepishly at me, and checked around to see if anyone was watching. Once he was certain we were alone, he shook my hand and thanked me for not coming back to his cafeteria as he had been asked by several of his regular customers to ban me as I was putting them off their food! I couldn't answer and instead walked away in silence, all the time wishing I had the strength and confidence to tell him how offensive I found such talk and behaviour.

Fred had no idea he had offended me, it was as though he and most other white people believed that black people were lesser mortals and knew themselves to be inferior. I have to say that when his establishment closed down (due to lack of trade) a few years later, I felt little in the way of sympathy for him.

Another place I would visit never handed over any change. Whenever I paid for a cup of tea or coffee, or a meal, they would take my money and keep it. When I asked for the change they would forcefully tell me that

I had already been given it. This happened to me a few times before I realised they were forcing me away from using their business. It was all very difficult and confusing to me.

At Elland Road on a match day or during training, the white man was welcoming and embraced my presence in the Leeds team, yet once I was out of that environment I became a social enemy. It was as though I was viewed as some kind of infectious disease, and being associated with me or having me on their premises was seen as a kind of stigma. It was a lonely existence, and for a long time it did force me to stay within my own comfort zone, mainly within the Beeston district.

There was no one I could tell or speak to about it. Certainly, Don Revie didn't want to know. I approached him in those early days and asked how I could combat and overcome the skin colour issue that existed. His response wasn't particularly good or what I was hoping for. He told me it was my own problem, an issue I was to address myself. He made the comment that if I had 'hang ups' about being different and about my skin colour, then maybe I should be looking to more involvement with black-only communities. I explained that I didn't have 'hang ups' and that in my opinion it was some of the white people who had 'hang ups' about black people. He said I was talking rubbish and that the white people had lived in harmony for centuries. It was down to me, as a black person from another country, to ingratiate myself with them, and to conform to their social ways.

He wasn't being malicious, just disrespectful really. Perhaps my timing of such a discussion wasn't good, he was clearly too wrapped up in forging his own managerial career to worry about my social concerns. His parting words on the matter were, 'Don't let all this nonsense affect your game, you are here for one reason, to play football, and that's all that the people of Leeds care about where you are concerned, Albert, how you perform on the football pitch. If people are rude to you, don't go to the places where that sort of thing happens again.' It was poor advice and left me feeling alienated in the city.

There were just three games left for the club to secure their division two status, it was perhaps fortunate that the teams struggling around them were consistently failing, helpful to the club just above the relegation zone. Albert didn't really understand the concept of relegation through the football leagues, he realised that he was part of a team and after the brief discussion with the manager, he elected to keep his head down and make no comment about the different social and class structures that were evident across Leeds. He focused on the football and doing well for the team and its supporters.

Gerry Francis didn't feature for us the rest of that season, a situation which seemed to cause him concern. He desperately wanted a decent run in the team alongside me, and a chance to improve both our games. He had played in many games that season, the vast majority when Jack Taylor was manager, but it seemed that Don Revie wasn't overly impressed with him, as he played him just the once, in the game at Stoke City.

A few players in the club were surprised that Gerry wasn't given a chance, but things had become so competitive, that someone else's disappointment at being dropped or falling out of favour, was seized upon by certain players as a chance to move up the pecking order. I really didn't like those types of internal politics and wranglings. In my opinion, Gerry was being efficiently frozen out by certain elements within the club.

I now know from my own experiences, that if other players or staff want to do it, any footballer can be ostracised, and made to feel like an outsider. In training, passes would consistently be played too hard or deliberately made difficult for the selected player, in an attempt to show them up. Another method would be to ignore the player completely, in training or in actual games. He would be given no opportunity to shine and effectively ignored. I'm not saying that happened to Gerry, but, again from experience, I know there were ill-educated people within the football club who weren't open to having black players representing them out on the pitch.

The following game against Lincoln City was like a walk in the park, they were a beaten team before they even set foot on the Elland Road pitch. Some of their players were discussing wages and transfers with us before the game. They seemed indifferent to the fact that they were going to be relegated and playing at a lower standard.

I asked one player if he was concerned that it may reflect on his career and future if the team was relegated. I was stunned to hear him say in response, that it was just a job and nothing to get worked up about. He told me that personally, he was a winner, and once the season was over he would find himself a 'better paying' club during the summer break. I couldn't believe the terrible attitude, he didn't care or concern himself how it might affect the Lincoln City supporters. It was all about him, no one else, just him!

I kept my eye out for him during the game, he strolled about the pitch as though he hadn't a care in the world. We comfortably hammered Lincoln 7–0, virtually sealing their relegation, there was no fight in their game and when the final whistle blew they seemed to put much more effort in getting off the pitch than they did throughout the game.

Afterwards, I saw the Lincoln player I had spoken to pre-match. Jokingly, I said that he wasn't a winner today. He turned sharply, looked at me and shouted, 'Fuck off, nigger boy, I'll always be more of a winner than you ever will be, I'm no blackie!'

The win we had over Lincoln City meant we would be again playing in division two the next season and there was a much relief around the club. The chairman was pleased with our performances since Don Revie had taken over and came to the changing room area to see and thank us. The boss himself wasn't overly enthused by the performance, he was looking beyond the number of goals we had scored, and identifying positions in the team that required attention and strengthening. We were told that we had to continue to work hard and that we would be fighting for our places next season, in the remaining two games.

I was a bit worried by this statement, but Grenville assured me that Don Revie was reminding those players who thought because we were safe with two games to go, that it was job done for the season and they could switch off.

A few days later we managed a 2–2 draw with Scunthorpe United, before losing our last game of the season at Charlton Athletic 2–0. For the last two games of the season, Terry Carling took over in goal. He was a hard working and solid sort of goalkeeper who had been at the club for a few years (1956) before getting his initial first team opportunity in April 1960. I wasn't the manager, nor was I looking to be, but for whatever reason, Terry never really established himself in Don Revie's good books and wasn't in my opinion given a fair chance to show his worth. It seemed fairly obvious that the boss believed the goals we were conceding were down to goalkeeping errors as opposed to bad defending.

Terry was another player, like Gerry Francis, who seemed to be on the peripheries of the first team but always played a bit part. It was something I found hard to understand, the constant swapping and changing of the first team meant that players were never comfortable and therefore in some cases, saw others playing in the same role, as threats. It upset the balance and understanding of our play, certainly my own game suffered in those early days, because of the constant uncertainty at the club. I had only been in Leeds for four months, and already I had played for two different managers and was aware that two players were already coveting my own position. Colin

Grainger, 'the singing winger' or 'the singing footballer' as he was better known, because he had an excellent singing voice and often performed at theatres and playhouses to large audiences, had been a virtual ever present the season I joined, and when he was out he was replaced by John Hawksby, who I replaced on the left wing.

Both players were full of confidence, Colin in particular had a playing career elsewhere and had experience with Sheffield United and Sunderland before being bought by Leeds. He had played for England, scoring on his debut against Brazil. John had come through the youth ranks and had played for England youth. He broke into the first team managed by Jack Taylor, and had scored on his debut and in the following game. He was well liked and some people at the club were forever reminding me what an outstanding talent he was.

Having two players challenging for my own position added to my insecurity. I tried my best to put the matter out of my thoughts, but the competitive spirit throughout the playing ranks constantly played on my mind and it wasn't aided by the way I was being treated away from football. I needed to go home to South Africa and be amongst my own family in a place I could relax.

\* \* \* \* \*

The season over, I was given dispensation by Don Revie to go home for a short break during the summer, on the absolute promise that I would come back to Leeds. I saw that as a good sign that I had a future at the club.

Going back to South Africa was strange, I had established English habits, drinking tea and becoming accustomed to the climate and weather. When I returned home, it wasn't quite the same as I expected it to be. Everyone was thrilled at my apparent success and I recounted so many stories of how wonderful it was that I began to believe them myself. I didn't want my family to know how upsetting it was, being tormented because of my colour across England. I needed them to feel comfortable in the knowledge that I was achieving. The reality was very much different.

The break allowed me to think of new ways to settle and get involved with the people of Leeds, I wanted to impress them with my football skills, but I also wanted them to see me as someone who wasn't different.

This was no easy thing for Albert to do, especially as the political and social environment of the Western world was in 1961, racially volatile. In America for instance, in a bid to combat segregation on public transport, a group known as the Freedom Riders (consisting of seven black and six white people) boarded two Greyhound buses in Washington DC, and headed south to New Orleans. The Civil Rights leader, Martin Luther King supported the Rider's efforts, and publicly spoke out for change and the cessation of segregation.

In Anniston, one of the buses was firebombed and subjected to an attack by members of the white supremacists, the Ku Klux Clan. The mob violence had been organised by local senior police officers who stood by and watched the attack unfold. A hospital where many of the injured Freedom Riders were taken refused to treat them and ejected them onto the streets in the early hours of the morning. The abandoned group were rescued from further beatings by local black activists.

The second Freedom Riders bus was ambushed and the occupants attacked in Birmingham, Alabama, when Ku Klux Klan members, supported and aided by the police, attacked activists with iron pipes, baseball bats and bicycle chains. Such matters were avidly reported in newspapers across the globe, politicians spoke out and many shamefully became involved in matters which were of no relevance to British society. In many instances, this inflamed cultural animosity, and reckless speeches and comments incited further racially-motivated activity across the country where Albert now found himself, England.

# 7

# Finding Love in Leeds

My life in Leeds was gradually improving as I settled myself down to a brand new season and what I saw as a 'fresh start' at the football club. To be a part of the club at the outset of a new season with a manager who was desperate to impress and achieve, was, I believed, a good time to be involved and Leeds was great place to be.

On my return to England, I went to the stadium to speak with Don Revie. I wanted to let him know that I was back in Leeds, and that I was ready to go and get into training. I also wanted to thank him for giving me the opportunity and to reassure him I was up for the challenge ahead and very much looking forward to playing alongside Gerry Francis in the coming months and showing the world how good we were.

I didn't get the reception or response I anticipated from my visit. Don Revie was clearly put out by my impromptu attendance and told me that he didn't give a damn about hearing my promises, he wanted to see positive action on the pitch. He said it was arrogant of me to come to him expecting to be playing every week and alongside another South African!

I was stunned by the outburst and before I could say anything else I was advised that, unless it was prearranged or by invite, I wasn't just to turn up at his office and waste his precious time with such ridiculous matters that he wasn't interested in. He really put me in my place. I apologised and left, returning to my room in Noster Hill.

It was lesson learned. During the period of my trial I had sensed that Don Revie was indifferent and displayed an aloofness towards me. Now, after this outburst, I felt alienated and that he was unapproachable, at least to me anyway. Other players seemed to have a good connection and open contact with him, but not me. I spoke to some of the other players about the manager's attitude towards me, each one told me something different. Grenville Hair advised me to keep my own counsel and not to speak out to other players about the manager as there was a 'select few' who would not hesitate to let him know and elaborate on what I said.

It wasn't the most positive return to football or to England, yet the experience offered me an insight into how serious the manager took his position and how he viewed his relationship with me. I opted to do as he asked, not to bother him with trivialities and promises, but to deliver in my performances.

I detected a certain unease at the football club, a nervousness in certain players that another tough season lay ahead in which the fight for places would be even greater. We all wanted the stability that a confirmed place in the starting eleven provides, but there were maybe just half a dozen players who could feel so confident, the rest of us were left to battle it out between us. That, so far as I could see, meant at tussle between me, Colin Grainger and John Hawksby.

Away from football, I began to gain an understanding of the local culture and how the different communities lived their lives. Although it wasn't openly stated, there were certain no-go areas for black people in Leeds and Roundhay and Oakwood were two places I never felt comfortable in. There was a bitterness shown towards me and while many people just ignored my presence, others reacted badly and without any provocation.

One incident I remember took place about this same time. I had been walking in Roundhay Park, and called into a newsagent's shop which was nearby on Roundhay Road. As I walked in I remember seeing a look of shock on the shopkeeper's face. When I approached the counter, the shopkeeper refused to serve me and demanded I get out of his shop. Before I could react, two white men, both were what I would describe as middle-aged customers, physically manhandled me off the premises and threw me out onto the pavement. I still had the chocolate in my hand that I was going to pay for. I went to the shop door in an attempt to return it, but was shouted at and told to 'go away' by the men inside.

As I walked down Roundhay Road, a police car pulled up alongside me. A policeman got out and asked me where I had been? Where I was going? And who I was? When I explained, he told me to jump in the car and he would take me home.

During the journey he told me to be careful about where I went in the city as there were unsafe areas for people who were not from this country! 'Best to stick to your own kind, Albert' he advised me.

It was frustrating being treated like a third class citizen in a city and country which was supposed to be more socially advanced than South Africa.

From a football status, I was happy that my pre-season training went well, and I made the starting eleven on the opening day of the season at Charlton Athletic in London. We won the game 1–0 but it wasn't a pretty performance from me. Afterwards, Don Revie was full of compliments for my game, telling me that I had defended and attacked well. I was slightly confused by his tactics because he told me that I had to hang onto the ball for longer periods and not always get it into the penalty area as I had previously been told.

I started the first seven games of the season, we won the first two, but to be fair, we were a struggling side. After a run of three straight defeats, I was dropped by Don Revie. I had picked up a couple of knocks in a game at Sunderland and had been given a torrid time by the crowd who continually chanted Zulu warrior sounds at me throughout. The players were little better, an ill-educated group who unnecessarily used expletives alongside some of the strongest and most unethical challenges I had ever encountered on a sports field. We lost the game 2–1 and it was clear that I was being made the scapegoat for the poor run of form.

Don Revie pulled me to one side after the game and told me that he thought my mind wasn't on the game, and I wasn't the footballer he had been told I was. Apparently, I didn't track back and defend or challenge the right player when we were under pressure. I was speechless, other players had put in little effort, but it was me who was taking the brunt of the blame. I tried to explain that no other player in the team suffered the constant barracking from the crowd every week, and it was getting to me because it was never ending. His response to this was to tell me I was making excuses. He believed the knocks I had taken in recent games were as a result of me not concentrating and doing the things I had been told to do. I tried to tell him that he was wrong, but he told me that he was giving me a break, a rest, time to reflect on what I actually wanted. Once I had done that, then I was to go back to him to let him know how I planned to make progress. I cried. He showed no empathy towards my situation and instead of advising, he told me to pull myself together and sort myself out! It was an awful feeling, I felt alone. In hindsight, I lost a lot of faith in Don Revie that day.

It was a real struggle trying to cope with the prospect of failure, and with no one by my side to help and support me through this time, I considered turning my back on Leeds and going home to South Africa. Mrs Wineley was one of the few people who recognised my personal crisis. She made sure that my life in Noster Hill was as comfortable as it possibly could be.

Another good person who I had around me about this time was a local lad called Clive Middlemass. What a great man he is! Clive was a very determined full back. He stayed in the clubhouse in Noster Hill and he really kept my spirits high. He got me focusing on the positive things in my life, and it wasn't really a surprise to me when after his playing days were over, he became a manager. He is one of the few people in football who I could rely upon to give me the right advice.

I was sad to learn that he had suffered so much from the wrath of football fans in Carlisle. From what I heard they gave him a terrible time and he suffered a lot of abuse. I know how that feels, it's a lonely place to be, so I have much sympathy for him. I tried a couple of times to call the Carlisle club to speak with him. I left messages for him to get back in touch, but they don't appear to have ever been passed to him.

In 1990 the author interviewed Clive Middlemass during his management time at Brunton Park, Carlisle. At the time the football club were on the ascent, having suffered quick relegation from the second division to the fourth. Clive Middlemass, with no funds, had somehow stopped the slide and had managed to transform the team into potential promotion challengers, the club missing out on the play-offs through goal difference only, a 5–2 hammering at fellow promotion contenders, Maidstone United on the final day of the 1989/90 season costing them dearly.

The following season saw a demise in fortunes, with the club struggling financially. On the field performances failed to equal that of the previous campaign. The team toiled in the fourth division relegation zone, however, Clive was able to keep them in the football league, finishing the season eight points above the non-league drop zone. It was an incredible feat considering Carlisle's attendances were dire and he had received little or no financial support to help resolve problems. It was no secret in football that this was a club in decline. Had it not been for the experience and tactical awareness of Clive Middlemass, the club would have dropped out of the Football League long before it ever did.

During my occasional journalistic visits to Brunton Park,

I witnessed some of the dreadful abuse directed towards the manager as he stood by his dugout in front of the home terracing. Quite how he wasn't influenced by some of the vitriolic name calling directed towards him I do not know. Anywhere else, the offenders would be properly dealt with, yet inside a football stadium it is somehow believed to be socially acceptable and people laugh or ignore it. That doesn't help the victim towards who the abuse is hurled.

I asked Clive Middlemass how this made him feel and about his time at Leeds with Don Revie and especially, Albert Johanneson:

The fans react because they are passionate, I understand that, I do my best to try to keep them onside and send them home happy with a display of decent football and a good result, but at this level it's very hard. I've had to dig as deep as I ever have to get this group of players together and performing with any confidence.

They aren't the best footballers in the world, but they are honest lads and men trying to earn a living and make themselves successful. I won't deny, the names I get called do hurt, sometimes it is constant, at other times, those same people celebrate a good goal or great team effort alongside me. Football is such an emotive game, it brings the best and worst out of people sometimes.

You talk about Albert Johanneson, he's a great lad, but the abuse I take isn't anything like that Albert suffered when he was playing. Albert took abuse everywhere he went in football, I used to feel terrible for him, worse still was hearing everyday people in the street making crude remarks and comments.

To his credit, he did all he could to ignore the remarks, he tried not to get involved with the whole racism bit, he suffered it in silence, but he never accepted it. Who would? He did all he could to get on with his life without causing a fuss. It can't have been easy for him seeing other people in the same career, treated so differently because of the colour of their skin. The Albert I knew back then was a man who loved music, loved to dance, sing and eat spicy curry. He always kept himself fit and there aren't many people who could say they could beat him in cross-country races or in any running exercise. He was electric: the Black Flash is an apt name for him. If things had gone right for him, he could have had a glittering football career.

Such comments about Albert's reluctance to speak out weren't unique. In 1996 I carried out one of several telephone interviews with the now 'late' black footballer, Justin Fashanu. As a footballer, he had endured a massive amount of pressure when he became Britain's first £1 million black player. There followed further pressures when he also declared himself gay. The insular society of professional football didn't know how to deal with such matters. Fashanu had shown honesty and openness.

In return, because he was gay, one manager, Brian Clough allegedly, wouldn't allow him to train with the other players, treating him like an outcast. Fashanu's career spiralled downwards as he dropped from the glamorous media limelight and found himself the subject of rumour and speculation. He explained to me how lonely a game professional football is and how there is no network of support:

> The only closeness and honesty you can ever get generally comes from within your own family. Football, in general, doesn't know how to deal with black player abuse or racism, whatever package the politicians or football powers wish to disguise it as. Managers, players and even referees make unkind comments about everything from my skin colour, to my sexuality.
>
> I've tried to speak to people in the game about it, the Professional Footballers Association for example, dismissed my comments and told me that it was rare

that they have such complaints from their members. One high profile official told me I had to accept it. If I wasn't thick skinned enough to deal with it, and ignore it, then I should look at pursuing a different career.

In the end I couldn't trust many in the game, I have a few people I would call football friends but it was obvious that the issues I faced were something I had to deal with myself. In the end, I sought assistance and support elsewhere, outside of the game. That's why I say family support is so important in such situations. You should be able to rely on your family, you have a natural bond and connection.

My brother John suffers abuse about not only being black but because of me also. It as though people look for negative reasons to despise black people and footballers. I cannot imagine what it must have been like for Albert Johanneson in the 1960s. They claim society and life has improved since then, but I'm not so certain we have rid ourselves of racism. He must have been so strong and focused to deal with some of things that he was called, and the treatment he received from people in the game. Those should have been his own people who he could rely on.

I have seen videos of Albert in his playing days. He had sensational speed and ball skill, he was something special, but because he received little support and the abuse was allowed to continue, he lost confidence, direction and focus. There was no one there to help him. It's all very well holding fund raising events to give him financial backing. That's not what Albert needed, he needed moral and physical support to help him sort himself out and goals and aims for the future.

The Leeds team of Albert's time was heavily committed to winning at all costs, that's what the manager had indoctrinated into them. At every football club, players fall by the wayside, and for a variety of reasons drop out of the game. When Albert dropped out of the game over here, (in the early 1970s) Leeds were achieving their ambitions; they were regarded as a winning club. Albert was all but a forgotten man, another footballer discarded onto the soccer scrapheap.

Don Revie and Leeds United may well have felt that they had fulfilled their obligations to him. They provided him with his football opportunity over in England, and he had served them well but as always, new talent comes along and suddenly his playing services were no longer required.

I was saddened when I heard of his death. I met and spoke with him a couple of times, and he was a kind and gentle man, unassuming and respectful of others. I believe that as a trailblazing black footballer, football let him down, people in football failed him. They can all say that we tried, we held fundraisers, subsidised him with gifts of financial support, but what they probably didn't understand was that Albert wanted something that is free: friendship, not sympathy or bitterness. Like me, he wanted to be treated as an equal. Not maligned or the subject of negative attention, all that does is send you further down the wrong path.

As far as I'm concerned, Albert Johanneson should be recognised as a hero, a man who battled and had to experience blatant racism that is far worse than any other footballer ever has or, in all likelihood ever will. We shouldn't just dismiss what he did and achieved in a few sentences. Every footballer playing in Britain should be reminded of the perils and dangers of racism, how it destroys innocent people, families and lives.

It's a poignant reminder to everyone connected to present day football: officials, managers, players and fans alike, that racism is not at all pleasant, clever or a solution, it is 100 per cent destructive. I agree with the late Justin Fashanu that football hasn't dealt with such problems. One doesn't have to search very far to find the existence of racism in the game. It's everywhere, from ill-phrased comments made by FIFA officials, to reckless public comments made by television pundits, to managers abusing their fellows.

I was fortunate enough to know and interview several times, Keith Alexander, who is perhaps one of the most successful and highly regarded black football managers in the British game. Keith told me how he knew and respected Albert Johanneson for all he did.

Albert for me, was a real inspiration. One of the first things I did when I was able, was to look him up and speak to him. I was playing for Kettering Town at the time and happened to know someone who knew him.

When I met him he wasn't in the best of health, yet he took the time to talk to me and give me advice, not only on football matters but how to deal with some of the problems he had endured in the game. He embraced me with a bear-type hug and laughingly, told me I was a 'lanky awkward looking bugger.'

His life hadn't been a bed of roses, that's for sure, and some of the things he told me about his time in the game made me cringe. Despite that he seemed to see it as a learning curve in his own life. He talked of professional regrets, his biggest one being his failure to keep a regular place in the Leeds team. He told me he had been forced or pushed out of the club because he didn't conform to the manager's way of playing or thinking and I think he had been termed a 'black sheep' by one of the club's directors, which, you would hope was nothing more than an unfortunate turn of phrase. He said that some people in the club had never accepted him as a black person and when he mentioned this to the manager, he received no help and slowly began to feel excluded. Yet he spoke of Leeds United with great affection.

There is no doubt that he loved the club but at the same time one cannot help but feel that some people in the club failed him in so many ways. I'm not suggesting it was deliberate, because I doubt anyone could recognise how tough it was for Albert. The fact is, he had no one in football he could turn to. Players he liked moved on to other clubs and Albert, was more or less abandoned, brought out for the odd game here and there but nothing that could lift his morale or give him hope that his career wasn't slipping away.

We can pontificate for hours, looking to apportion blame for what happened to him, but there are no answers; there was no understanding of how racial abuse affected individuals back in Albert's era. In all probability, he was viewed as something of a novelty, and not as an equal or a fellow human being.

Black footballers in the game back then were scarce, I can maybe name three or four, but Albert was the most successful and high profile of them all. There is only so much pain a human can take before it takes some kind of negative effect. Albert had nobody who could understand the pressure of football, or anyone to talk it through with. He dealt with it in the only way he thought possible, and sadly, he never recovered from that course of action.

He is a man I will always respect for a variety of reasons. Forget what's been said about him not being strong enough to handle the British game, Albert was stronger than most, he had to put up with much more than any of those footballers he played alongside ever did. Instead of dismissing his part in that team, Albert should be revered for his courage and bravery. Each and every time he pulled on the Leeds' football kit he was tormented, it takes someone very special to survive that kind of treatment for over a decade. I know how upsetting it is when other managers call me racist names, unlike Albert I react, I confront and ask what example they believe they are setting for other players and fans who often hear the crude comments.

British football and society needs to be educated, not preached to as so many government 'do gooders' do, about the negative influences racism has on the human race. We call ourselves a developing country, but governments are misguided. We haven't socially developed at all while racism openly exists, and it does. The days of apartheid and racial segregation should be relegated to the pages of history, not perpetuated in football in the 21st century.

Back at Leeds United, Albert may have felt much more comfortable when one of the players in contention for his position, Colin Grainger, left the club and moved to Port Vale in the October of 1961. Sadly for Albert, another of his colleagues who left the club, Gerry Francis, was seen as being surplus to requirements and sold by Don Revie to York City.

When Gerry left I felt more vulnerable than I ever had at the club. Gerry was one of the few people who knew what it was like being a black footballer in a white country. I think his transfer affected me more than it did him, and it wasn't helped by the fact that I had lost my place in the team and the games I was now featuring in were rarely watched by the manager. My aspirations of having a full season to settle in and progress were in tatters. I felt certain that with Gerry gone, I would soon be following him out of the same exit door.

First team selection became more and more scarce, and on the few occasions I did manage to get a game, it was mainly due to an injury or knock sustained by my replacement on the left wing, John Hawksby. It's wrong, I shouldn't call him a replacement because he wasn't. In the manager's opinion he was worthy of his place in the first team.

One highlight of that football season was scoring my first-ever goal for the club. It was a penalty kick in a League Cup game at Elland Road against Rotherham United. We lost 2-1, and scoring from the penalty spot isn't always seen as a spectacular or skill-orientated goal, but it was special for me because it was my first. It was met with little in the way of celebration but remains a personal milestone of my career.

Another goal I scored that season came at Newcastle in the final game of the season. I remember turning two or three Newcastle defenders and hearing them call me terrible names. Generally, I took this sort of treatment from a player, as a sign that I had created a chance and had left them behind and embarrassed. I put my foot through the ball and blasted past the Newcastle goalkeeper and into the goal. It felt as though it was a good goal to score. I expressed my ability well in that game because I had a hand in every goal we scored (3–0 win), even the own goal Newcastle scored as I recall.

Afterwards, I was in great demand. Journalists wanted to speak to me and people associated with both the Newcastle and Leeds clubs congratulated me on an excellent all-round performance. Syd Owen told me that my display had singlehandedly saved Leeds from relegation. Once again, I felt as though people were recognising me as a talented footballer and therefore I hoped would see me as more of an equal away from the game.

If someone was to ask me what the favourite years of my life are, I would have to say that 1962 was special, not only for football reasons, but because it was the year I fell in love with a beautiful woman. She is the greatest woman I have ever had in my life. Her name was Norma Elaine Comrie. She was a couple of years younger than me, but the instant we met, I knew she was the right and only woman for me.

Norma and her family lived at 21 Stonegate Street in Leeds. She was what was termed a hospital dispenser, (better known as a chemist) and she made me so happy. I'm not comfortable discussing my family life, because that part of my life remains private to me and them only. but as with all families there was much love and some pain. I say 'them' because I married Norma at Blenheim Chapel in Woodhouse, on Wednesday, 27 February 1963 and we later had a family. My two beautiful little girls will forever be my own Princesses. Their good looks come from my wife and not from me.

The club seemed pleased that I had made some roots in the city and it was as though many people saw this as confirmation of my commitment to Leeds. It was a wonderful period of my life and it felt good that we were able to hold our wedding reception at a city centre hotel. Many of my football colleagues could attend since it took place on a Wednesday and due to a period of bad weather, football matches were being postponed. I think it was the first-ever black wedding that had more white guests in attendance than black.

It was a memorable day and Grenville Hair was beside me, supporting me throughout, until, as groom, it came to me giving my own announcements of appreciation. I was so nervous that I was shaking. Public speaking was not my greatest asset or skill. I was glad when the speaking part was over and was appreciative of family help in getting through it.

Inside I felt content, I had married a wonderful woman, and was achieving greater things in my football career. I made 44 appearances in that season, and scored 14 goals. The legendary John Charles had returned to the club and had instantly took a liking to me and tended to look after me. Having such a gracious and well respected footballer like that backing you and giving you advice was something I could only dream of.

John always told me to watch my back inside football, and to do what was right for me and no one else. 'Be selfish, you only get one chance at this game Albert,' he told me, 'there are bastards everywhere who will denounce you, trust no one who won't look you in the eye or buy you a beer, and always put yourself first. People, and I'm including football people, may shake your hand and talk at you, but do they talk to you? Do they listen to you? It's important to recognise that fact Albert, you are a skilful footballer, that is a rare commodity in this day and age, and especially so in division two. Life can shit on you if you don't remain vigilant and watch your own back. There is no such thing as a football family, it's a sport where only the strong survive and prosper.'

At the time, John's advice seemed out of place and I didn't really recognise what he meant. Now, in hindsight, I can clearly see what he meant, people used and trampled on me to get to where they wanted to be. As a footballer at Leeds United, I became a something, an object that some people used, an association with to look after themselves. In other more football related instances, they exploited my human weaknesses and used these as a lever to enhance their own careers. Putting it bluntly, as John Charles warned, they shit on me.

People who I regarded as friends at the football club were fast disappearing: Gerry Francis had gone to York City, John McCole had gone to America, and Peter McConnell and Terry Carling followed Tommy Murray and were moved on to Carlisle. Derek Mayers, a right winger, lasted just one season before being sold to Bury.

There was a lot of movement in and out of the club, and it was clear that the manager was bringing in tougher more experienced players to help strengthen the side. He was determined to make Leeds into a robust side, with players who wouldn't back away from a rough challenge. Players like Bobby Collins and Willie Bell were two of the most notable signings. Bobby Collins stands alongside Billy Bremner as the toughest footballers I know. They have many things in common, both are Scottish and very proud, both are without fear, both are leaders, both are winners, and both were excellent footballers. Nice men whose personality and demeanour changed once they went out onto the football pitch, where they transformed into their alter egos, unleashed wild animals whose aim was to win every ball and challenge.

It was great for me having two such players in the same team. They covered every blade of grass and fed me the ball every time they broke from defence. It isn't without coincidence that my play and appearances improved when they played together. None of us knew at the time, that as a club, we were destined for even greater achievements.

# 8

# A Claim to Fame

My life felt more complete now that I had my own home and a wonderful wife and locally based family to rely upon. Our home was in a good part of Leeds, allowing some degree of privacy and tranquility from the outside world. I do believe that Norma's support helped me focus on my game much more than I had previously. Consistency was key to my confidence, I needed to be in the first team to help with my self-belief.

The 1962–1963 season was another good one for me and the club, I missed just one league game after literally being kicked off the Elland Road pitch against Sunderland. It was obvious that I was targeted for abuse by the Sunderland players from the moment the first ball was kicked.

The game was probably in its second minute and I was nowhere near the ball when I was punched in the back of the head and called a 'darkie' by a Sunderland player. A few minutes later, during a challenge, I had my knee deliberately stamped on, the pain was shocking and I yelled out. The referee ran over and told me not to be so soft and to get to my feet. My knee swelled up like a tiny balloon, but I played on because if I left the pitch we would be at a disadvantage. The entire game was marred for me by Sunderland's rough tactics; no other player was targeted like I was.

Afterwards, the Sunderland manager Alan Brown came to see me. He apologised for the 'kicking' his lads had given me throughout the game. 'I didn't honestly think you'd stand up to it, but you did, so all credit lad, judging by today's performance, I'm certain that Revie will soon knock the football out of your game though. If you fancy getting out of this place and coming to Sunderland then let me know, I'll make you a better player than you ever thought you could be.'

The conversation took me by surprise, and there was something about the man that made me believe that he meant what he said. I took it as a compliment that he had identified me as sufficiently a threat that needed to be stopped by hurting me. It also showed me that there existed no 'on the field' respect in football, especially between players and managers. For a few moments I considered what Alan Brown said about a move to Sunderland, then dismissed it because I loved Leeds and all that it was providing me: a family, a home, money and a reasonable lifestyle. Notwithstanding, I really enjoyed playing for Leeds United and I intended to be loyal to the club and to the people of the city who followed the team.

The season was barely a few weeks old when John Charles left the club and was again sold. John's departure felt like I had lost someone who understood me and recognised my strengths and weaknesses. What followed was unbelievable success. A season later we won the Second Division Championship and I received my first medal in English football. Despite my reservations about Don Revie's ruthless style of football, it was working for me and I was thoroughly loving my game.

The season was spoiled for me when the boss dropped me for a game at Sunderland, because, he said, I was too weak for a team like Sunderland and I would be bullied by their players. It was put about that I was injured, but the knock I had sustained wasn't anything like serious enough to prevent me from playing. I was angry and upset by the manager's reaction, it wasn't the first time I ever took drink, but this time I went out and drowned my sorrows with alcohol. I felt rough for several days later and vowed never to drink again. Thankfully, common sense prevailed and I was returned to the team after missing that one game.

Its often been said by some of his peers that Albert wasn't good enough and couldn't cope with the pressures and style of first division football. I have never been a supporter of such a notion, I always have and, knowing Albert as I did, I continue to disagree with such statements.

There is no real evidence to support the purely anecdotal theory that he just wasn't good enough at the higher level of the game. It is a select few who regurgitate this claim and statistics dictate details and facts to the contrary. Albert featured in a total of 36 league and cup games that season, scoring a total of 12 goals. That's as good a return as any other player in that same side and he was the club's second top goalscorer.

Throughout the season, he showed his capability to compete with the very best in the English game, and it was regularly recorded in the press that he ran defenders ragged with his devastating pace and trickery. Those sort of statistics and reviews are hardly conducive to a player who wasn't good enough and didn't have the courage and strength to compete in the first division.

After winning promotion I went back to South Africa in the summer months. I hadn't spent much time there in the years since I came to Leeds, and it felt good to be back there and to see everyone. But my future life was in Leeds and I spent much of my time planning what I wanted to achieve on my return to England.

I really enjoyed playing in that first season in division one. Our resilience was tested each week, and we showed with our football that we were able to challenge with the best players in the game.

One of my favourite games was beating Everton at Leeds. Some of the Everton players had been at me since they arrived at the stadium, calling me a 'nig-nog' and a 'golliwog' from the Black and White Minstrels show. It wasn't done discreetly either, it was done in public areas and was heard by many people, including Don Revie, who laughed at the comedy of the Black and White Minstrels comment. I told him I didn't like being called those sorts of names. He told me not to listen to them if I didn't like them, to ignore them.

I was feeling uptight before the game and had a word with Billy Bremner to let him know I was feeling angry at the boss and the Everton players. Billy put things in perspective for me, 'Don't you worry about name calling Albert, the boss doesn't mean any harm when he ignores it and says nothing to back you up. He is dismissing it for what it is, bloody nonsense, it's rubbish, remember what I once told you about using negative emotions positively. Well, why don't you do that today, get stuck into them and give them plenty of other things to call you by showing them up for what they are, useless.'

We won the game 4–1 and I scored two of the goals. There was one point early in the game when one of the Everton players called me a 'black bastard'. The referee was close at hand and heard the remark. I asked him if he was going to do something about it. 'Nothing son, that's what they think you are though, a black bastard, so why worry?'

I was angry and while the ball was out of play went to see Don Revie in the dugout and told him what had been said. The support wasn't there. 'Albert, what the bloody hell do you expect me to do about that? Get back out there and call him a 'white bastard.' If you do that you are both equal.'

I preferred Billy's advice and so used my skill to expose the opposition's weaknesses.

\* \* \* \* \*

That season also saw Leeds reach Wembley in the FA Cup Final; it was a genuine privilege to be part of that day. Few footballers get to play in a proper Cup Final at Wembley, let alone a black South African. So when I was named in the team to play against Liverpool I was initially thrilled. It was a major event for the city and the football club and in the week leading up to the game, we were all treated like royalty in the city.

It seemed as though everyone wanted a part of us, to speak with us and wish us well. There was no doubt in my heart that the football supporters of Leeds were behind me and saw me as one of them. I lost count of the number of autographs I signed that week. It was perhaps one of the best weeks of my football career, if not my life.

I enjoyed the thrill of being recognised for being a footballer and the style and lifestyle that brings: complimentary meals in restaurants, free drinks, countless compliments and much adulation.

On the day of the game, I felt my self-confidence draining from me when a journalist referred to me as the 'sambo' playing for Leeds. I heard it said, 'If he plays he will be the first ever black footballer to play in a Cup Final at Wembley. Who would have thought it? A man raised in filthy rat-infested slums now playing in the FA Cup Final.'

The words of John Charles filled my thoughts, 'You are a commodity.' It was clear that while other players appearing in the same game were individuals, I was represented as an object. I went to tell Don Revie to pull me out of the team because I wanted to protest and make a stand so people could see that what they were doing to me was wrong. He didn't want to hear about my feelings. 'Albert, what are you saying to me? This is the bloody FA Cup Final for Christ's sake, not many players get to do this, now you are telling me you don't want to because someone has called you a stupid bloody name. I'm not listening to you, you are capable of winning this game for us, that's why you are playing.'

Nothing that was said comforted me. I felt ill. I spent a lot of time in the bathroom, I was being sick and had diarrhoea. It was awful, my whole body was trembling and I just didn't feel like I could play. In the tunnel before we came out onto the pitch some of the Liverpool players got at me, calling me dreadful things. Ordinarily, I would have risen above this sort of behaviour, but it affected me. Billy and Jack Charlton retaliated in my defence, and had a go back at the players in question.

Then when we walked out onto the pitch all I could hear was a cacophony of Zulu-like noises coming from the terraces. It was dreadful, I could barely hear myself think for those screams. I wanted to run back down the tunnel, but, I filled my thoughts with how proud my entire family and friends would be at seeing me playing at Wembley.

The first time I received the ball out wide, I was met with a crunching tackle from one of the Liverpool defenders. This was followed by a couple of discreet punches to my kidneys. Sufficient to let me know that it was going to be rough game where I was concerned. The foul play continued throughout the game, long enough for some of my colleagues to bypass moves away from me. That further damaged my confidence.

The Wembley pitch was terrible, muddy and heavy. I couldn't get any of my runs going, and when I did find space, the state of the pitch with mud and divots took the ball away from me. I was completely out of sorts throughout the game and when the final whistle blew I was devastated that we had lost and with my performance. Yet, part of me was relieved it was all over.

The boss didn't really speak to me too much after the game. Les Cocker did his best to lift my confidence and told me not to worry. There would be other Wembley appearances for me to flourish and show off my skill, but the damage was done. It felt as though I had let down everyone who'd ever known me. If I am honest, my relationship with Don Revie was never the same after that game. I may have made black football history, but believe me when I tell you, I still look back on that game with much despair and sadness. If I could ever reverse time to have another chance to redeem myself, then I would want another opportunity to play at Wembley.

I again returned to South Africa during the summer,

and tried to find suitable solutions for coping with the racial abuse I was suffering in football. Don Revie had made it clear to me that he didn't want to know or hear about the issues of racism and had gone so far as to tell me that I was speaking untruths when I told him what was happening. It was difficult because I desperately wanted to respect Don Revie, but respect has to be earned, not commanded.

The following season the club made their intentions clear in signing Mike O'Grady from Huddersfield Town for £30,000. It was a very clear message to me that Revie didn't think I was good enough. He was finding it difficult to acknowledge my existence at the football club, let alone provide support and motivation, again that came from Les Cocker who told me to knuckle down and show the boss that I had what it takes to hold down the position of left winger.

I was dropped for the first few games of the season and only used on a handful of occasions in the league and cup. It was evident that that I was regarded as a fringe player and nothing more. The club, as an excuse for my non appearances, would tell the press that I was struggling with injuries when I really wasn't. It was all very confusing and of course my trust for certain people within the team was quickly disappearing. It was however, helpful that I made appearances in European competitions. By finishing as runners up in the league and FA Cup, we had qualified for the Inter Cities Fairs Cup competition and managed to reach the semi-final, where I scored against Real Zaragoza. That goal and those appearances gave me a lift, as some of the European football nights were highly charged and allowed us to further develop as a team.

The situation between myself and the manager was becoming almost intolerable, for me at least, he would only speak with me when I was selected for the first team or when I was in the treatment room, which tended to be more a more frequent occurrence as my position at the football club deteriorated. I had taken up smoking, some of the other players found it relaxing and the dressing room was often filled with cigarette or cigar smoke, so I was already a passive smoker. Not only that, I was enjoying a drink, sometimes only once or twice a week, but as I became more anxious by Don Revie's attitude towards me, I often drank every day. Neither habit was good for my football performance or health, and domestically, because I had taken up bad habits, I was squandering money. I didn't realise it at the time, but I had taken the first few steps towards oblivion.

Every so often I would pull myself back from the brink and deliver a great performance in training, causing the management to consider giving me an opportunity in the first team. I seemed to suit European football and put in my finest performances in such games. I scored my first hat-trick against DWS Amsterdam, and became the club's first player to score three goals in a European game. I managed to repeat the feat the next season, when we beat Spora Luxembourg 7–0.

In another game during 1967, I suffered serious damage to my knee ligaments. This kept me out of contention for a first team place and the injury never really did heal properly. My appearances were getting less and less as the season went by.

On the insistence of Les Cocker, my brother, Trevor, had a trial at the club around this same time, as did another South African footballer. Neither made the grade, one player left accusing Don Revie of being fundamentally unfair towards him.

Fans would ask why I wasn't playing and I could never honestly answer them, because I didn't know the answer. Albeit I did, it was because the manager had severed his ties with me. He had lost faith and used me when it suited. Some of the other players at the club would advise me to keep putting the effort in during training sessions, privately, some were surprised by my exclusion and told me it may be better if I looked for another club.

My problem was I loved living in Leeds and I felt

settled there. I didn't want to be regarded as a failure, yet that's how it felt. Don Revie was deliberately making me feel like that. I didn't want my family to know what I was experiencing as they would think I was weak. So with no one in football at Leeds to talk to who could understand the race issues I was suffering, I began to find friends through alcohol in the pubs and bars of Leeds.

Initially, when I began to visit city centre pubs I would be recognised, and it would get fed back to some of the other players who in turn would tell Don Revie. They didn't do it to be nasty, I think they thought they were helping me, so I began to use more inhospitable and environmentally unfriendly hostelries where people didn't visit to gossip but to drink.

My last game for Leeds United was against Burnley at Elland Road. I admit I wasn't in the best of ways, having been drinking until the early hours of the day of the game. It didn't help that Burnley kicked lumps out of me and were on my case from the kick off. No matter what I did, I seemed to end up being hacked to the floor or knocked off the ball. In the end I could take no more, I gave up, my knees gave way in the penalty area and I collapsed to the floor. I felt as though I was going to be sick through the affects of the alcohol.

As I lay on the floor, desperate to be taken off, I watched in awe as Eddie Gray displayed the kind of skill I once possessed; he weaved past six or seven Burnley players in the penalty area before scoring a great goal. It was an incredible goal, my heart sank as I realised that it could have been me receiving the celebrations at scoring such a wonder goal, instead, I was laid upon the floor feeling sorry for myself.

Nobody acknowledged my injury and I felt invisible as I was taken off the field. Don Revie gave me a dirty look when I walked past him, he uttered some comment that he was finished with me. I tried to say sorry to him, but he turned his back on me as though I did not exist.

Relations got so bad between the manager and myself

that I thought the only way I could communicate with him was by letter, so I penned a full apology for my behaviour and begged and pleaded with him to give me a further opportunity to prove myself. I received no reply, but for my efforts was rewarded by being placed on the transfer list.

I requested a meeting with the manager and was granted fifteen minutes in his office. I wanted to clear the air between us, he wanted me out of the club. Instead of sorting out the issues between us he told me that the club had accepted an offer from Bury and it was in my best interests to talk to them.

I feel embarrassed to say it, but I went down on my bended knees in front of him, and asked him not to release me. 'Get out of my office Albert, why are you doing this? You are a bloody disgrace, now get up off your knees and leave me in peace. You are finished here, your time is up, I told you never to let me down but you have too many times now. You're washed up, look at you. If you don't go to Bury then you will go somewhere else, there is little or no chance of you getting into my team now, I've got plans and you don't figure in them.'

I went to speak to Bury, it was a wrong move for me, I had a chat with a couple of other clubs, Brighton and Walsall, but nothing came of any of the talks.

In the summer of 1970, I eventually signed for York City who were in the fourth division. It was a fresh start and I was determined to seize it, but my life was already in a downward spiral. I had put on weight, lost fitness and with it went my pace and touch.

Life at York wasn't great, the crowds were much smaller therefore the racial abuse was much easier to hear as it wasn't drowned out by other chants. The standard of football was poor to say the least, yet my colleagues were supportive of my situation and did what they could to protect me from the regular terrace barracking.

The highlight of my career at York came in a cup game against Southampton when each and every one of us playing for York City battled and fought for every ball and we managed a 3–3 draw. I recognised that I had lost a lot of pace because I no longer left defenders in my wake; they were either fitter or I was slower. It was in this game that someone in the crowd called me a 'fat nigger' funnily enough, being called 'fat' really hurt me, equally as much as the racism.

Two years later, and it was all over. My football career crumbled to nothing, York released me because I wasn't fit enough, my weight was getting worse and my drinking habits were getting me into trouble. I wasn't what you could call a pleasant drunk, I often became outspoken towards management and staff. My life became a blur and because I was such a bastard in my ways, the one outstanding love I had in my life, my wife and children, I lost. I drove them away. I can never forgive myself for that, my beautiful wife and children were gone.

I made a final desperate bid to sort myself out and returned to South Africa. I signed for Glenville FC and stayed there for a season or so before returning to England, vowing to rebuild my football career. In that time football had moved on and so had life. I was without money so took to washing up chores in Chinese restaurants or anywhere that needed that sort of help. The people of the city never forgot who I was and still, whenever I go out, I need nothing but my bus fare. I am treated to drinks and food.

Gradually, I lost control of who I was, other people were making decisions for me, unscrupulous people abused my good name and I was associating with the wrong kind of person. It's difficult once you get into such a place to remove yourself from it and I often found myself in trouble with the law for my actions when in drink. I am not a bad person, nor am I deliberately belligerent, but at one time I was stumbling from one crisis to another, I felt alone and without any source of comfort other than that found in alcohol. Don Revie was right, I was washed up.

In 1993, after help from various non-footballing sources, Albert agreed to attend the Chaucer Clinic for addicts, then based in Southall, West London. He admitted he had a drink problem that required treatment and with positive testimonials of how the same clinic had helped another alcoholic footballer, Jimmy Greaves, he understood his situation and positively accepted the treatment and support. His counsellor at the clinic, Nicky de Villiers, worked closely with Albert and explained how serious and life threatening his condition was. Apparently, things were so bad that experts believed Albert's body could not take another serious bout of drinking and he was facing certain death if he continued to drink.

For a time Albert was in recovery, then came an invite to attend a bespoke fundraising event and testimonial in Leeds. Staff at the clinic did what they could to deter Albert from attending the event, but as his counsellor later stated, 'People here are not prisoners and can exercise their own free will.'

Albert attended the event, but his problems began earlier in the day. When he arrived in Leeds he had been met by well-wishers who not realising, unwittingly treated him to drinks. Albert's efforts and work with the staff at the Chaucer Clinic were undone with one drink.

The following day he called the clinic and explained his feeling of guilt at betraying all they had done for him. His counsellor went as far as to offer to come and fetch him from Leeds if he agreed to come back to Southall. Albert felt as though he had failed those same people and the friends he had made at the clinic. As a result, he didn't return.

No amount of reassurance could convince Albert in what were his latter days, that he was an absolute Leeds legend. There are many footballers who have been bestowed with such a title but rarely do they warrant it.

Albert, to the very end, remained a man of the people and the vast majority of people in Leeds loved him. He was open and honest in all he tried to achieve and despite being deliberately abused and downtrodden by society, in both South Africa and England, he survived and battled on. He never lacked courage, strength or conviction. He needed genuine friendship and support, someone to listen to him and help him have a voice. Outside his own family, he got none of that and so he dealt with things in the only way he could. Alcohol helped blur the abuse and fade the memory of all the suffering he had suffered and witnessed. He held no malice for anyone, not even Don Revie, the man he so desperately sought validation from, who rejected his desperate pleas and turned his back on him. He still regarded him as 'a great manager for Leeds United.'

It is sad that this great man whose early years were lived in the dictatorial world of South African apartheid, a boy and man who witnessed some of the vilest human atrocities imaginable, should find himself under the dictatorship at the English football club he saw as a solution to a degrading life of toil and woe he faced in the Wintersrand. Football is a wonderful sport, it allegedly brings together communities and unites countries of the world, yet if it is not managed properly it can be as destructive as any war. Racism, homophobia, hooliganism; all are attached to football. We hear every year from countless governments and police forces how the sport has been rid of such a disease. They are wrong, it merely hibernates and festers, before spawning a whole new generation of ill-educated people who use it as a weapon against others who can rarely retaliate.

Professional football across the world is suffocating under an abundance of reports of unacceptable accounts of racism. In 2012, the England international captain has to face charges in court of making racist comments to a black colleague and a high profile Premier League team supported a colleague who admitted and was found guilty of making a racist comment to another footballer. At the other end of the football spectrum, a non-league footballer has reported blatant racist abuse by another footballer. So what has changed since the 1960s when Albert had bananas thrown at him from the terraces and other players openly abused him? Racism isn't a crime that is solely the responsibility of football, it is everyone's personal responsibility to treat others equally and fairly.

Whether that is achievable remains to be seen. The recording of the life of Albert Johanneson will hopefully go some way to highlighting the negative issues it could lead to, if it is not correctly dealt with. Albert didn't deserve to suffer as he did. He doesn't deserve to be the forgotten man of Leeds United and football, and must be regarded as an inspiration to other minorities who aspire to achieve. Albert did it, he travelled halfway round the world and inspired a whole generation of football supporters in Leeds. His legacy remains for all to see; black footballers are very much part of the English game and are no longer seen as rarities, unique or novelties. Football is about people, every child and adult has a right to enjoy it, so let's embrace it and give a huge thank you to Albert Johanneson, the ambassador, husband, father, uncle, friend, who made the football bodies of the world sit up and take notice. He came, he saw, he conquered, we failed him. May his memory and achievement live on forever.

# 9

# Looking for Albert

My journey to find the real Albert Louis Johanneson has taken me around the globe, to places that Albert never visited and possibly didn't know existed. Certainly, I never expected to be speaking about Albert with a footballer in Haiti, or believed that his trailblazer reputation would have reached such a place. Yet it has and that player, who I know only as Benni, wanted to emulate Albert's professional success in the game.

I'm certain that Albert would be shocked and extremely overawed if he knew the high esteem in which he is held by the vast majority of sporting people and the public also. His legacy to black footballers everywhere can be witnessed up and down the football grounds of the United Kingdom and perhaps more so at the very highest level of the game, in the Premier League, where every club is represented by an overseas black footballer.

Albert certainly wasn't the first black footballer in the British game, but he was the first to play in a Wembley Cup Final and he was the first to play at a consistently high level. The ambassadorial status that has attached itself to him since his death is warranted, he was a trailblazer and despite what many suggest, he was brave and strong. What he lacked was professional support from individuals and organisations that should have done more. If that's taken as a criticism then so be it, however, it is obvious that Albert was failed not only by society but by the profession he fought so hard to achieve within professional football. In many respects, because of that failure, he has been allowed to become the forgotten man.

Like so many systemic failures it is far easier to forget than address such matters, it is only now, in more recent times that the reality of what Albert suffered throughout his time in the game can be openly talked about and discussed. Bodies such as Kick it Out, and Football Unites, Racism Divides, are doing a fantastic job in promoting equality in football and in trying to prevent racism. Albert would never have been a supporter or advocate of political correctness, which simply disguises prejudice in all its forms and ultimately forces it underground, he preferred honesty and integrity.

In many ways, in his latter years he was prosaic about racism within the United Kingdom:

> It exists, you cannot ever say it doesn't, I'm not only talking about white people on black, it's about black people on white as well. I'm sure that one day white people will become the minority in Britain and professional league football will see clubs field all black teams. It was never going to happen in my day, I was a novelty and some people have said that I was a luxury player that Leeds United didn't need. I can't say that anything in my life has ever been luxurious, least of all my football career, I worked hard to get to where I did but I fell out of favour with important people who made decisions that can make or break a career. I don't blame them as it was my doing as well, but when you are part of something special, then suddenly you are ignored, it's difficult. Being ignored made me feel different and unequal in terms of being a human. It was a form of abuse; perhaps I should have spoken out or stood up to the bullying but it's hard to do that when you are a part of a team and want to stay in that team.

I know that Albert was still suffering racial abuse in the

1990s, which tends to support the belief that things haven't changed too much since he first arrived on these shores.

On one occasion I was with him in Harrogate when a group of Asian youths hurled racist taunts at us both. We were sat on a bench, Albert wasn't feeling well and so I was comforting him as best I could. I was angered by the situation and stood up to confront the group, only for Albert to grab hold of my arm and tell me to 'leave it' and 'to ignore them.' The abuse continued for around two minutes and not even the threat of calling the police caused them to desist. Eventually they moved away and I was suitably chastised by Albert.

> If you show them that it affects you, then it will get worse and you get further abuse, and if they see you are vulnerable they will physically attack. That was a very stupid thing to do Paul, you should not have confronted a group like that.

I could see he was trembling, he was genuinely frightened. I asked if this kind of behaviour happened a lot.

> Sometimes it will be six or seven times a day, depending on where I am and what I am doing. If I'm inebriated, it gets worse and often I am beaten up and left in the gutter. I feel that many people see it as their right to kick, hit and spit on a black man sat in the street. I know it's wrong and I shouldn't be sitting in the street, but sometimes there is nowhere for me to go and I have no options. That shouldn't mean I deserve to be called names and set upon.

* * * * *

Like so many others, when I heard of Albert's death, I was stunned. I hadn't seen him for a few weeks. The last time we spoke was an interview for a magazine article. He hadn't been his usual chirpy self and that afternoon, he seemed down about many things in his life, speaking of his regrets and what he called 'tragedies' that caused him to change. I managed to lift his spirits with a bag of chips and curry sauce (I had previously learned that he loved a good curry) as we sat on a seat in Roundhay Park talking about South Africa, England, the city of Leeds and football. He was rambling about many different things. Primarily, he said he felt tired of everyday things, especially his life being such a struggle and a constant battle to survive.

> I look at black footballers today, they are doing alright for themselves, larger than life profiles, good money and playing for good clubs where any kind of playing association automatically brings respect without earning it. Footballers like Viv Anderson, he's done well for himself at Manchester and he's played for England as well. Imagine that in my day, a black man playing for England. I wouldn't have got anywhere near the England shirt back in the 1960s, not because I wasn't good enough, but because I am black.
>
> I remember Sir Stanley Matthews once telling me, 'You are a smashing footballer Albert, but you face a real challenge if you are to be regarded as being equal to your white colleagues. There are people in football, administrators, managers and players who won't like the thought of black players coming over here and showing off better skills. The football fraternity is complex and doesn't like change, you will be regarded as something of a novelty, an object of abuse. That's just the way football is over here. Your greatest challenge is not to prove your skill and ability, but to deal with and ignore what is said to you by football people and football fans, and how you will be treated. My advice to you is to look after Albert Johanneson and the things that are really important to you.'
>
> He was right on every count, I've been let down, failed

by some prominent people in football, and as a result I was given no support and jettisoned once they could see that I was beginning to struggle.

Eventually I lost my way and my life spiralled away from me. I'm not blaming anyone else for the problems I have, but there are people who know the truth, people who know how it was for me. It may not be popular or what you want to hear, but I was treated differently, and looking back now, I think quite badly and unfairly, by a man who is held in the highest regard by the people of Leeds. He really didn't want to know about anything where I was concerned, it was as though I didn't exist as part of his team. The players were supportive to me, but of the management, I can only say I felt abandoned.

I had my suspicions about the identity of who it was Albert felt let down by, yet felt uncomfortable in even considering that this person would make an orphan of one of my Elland Road heroes.

It was Mr Revie, Don Revie, he turned on me, ostracised me. On one occasion he walked past me in Leeds city centre. I saw him walking towards me on the same pavement, I held out my hand and presented it to him, I wanted to shake his hand. I needed him to acknowledge me, give me some validation that he had some respect for me. He pushed my hand away and brushed me aside as though I was a fly that he was swatting. I admit, I wasn't in the best of states appearance wise, nor was I sober, no matter, it didn't warrant treatment like that. I called out to him and reminded him that I was one of his family, his response was to turn and give me a cold blank stare that left me in no doubt that I no longer existed as part of his football family or in his world. That was the moment I understood that he held no respect for me.

As manager of the England national team, he never once gave a black footballer an international cap, maybe there was none worthy of a place in his side, I don't know. However, I was told by some other black players, that he, Mr Revie, had apparently commented that he was wary of black players because we were unreliable and uncommitted. He reckoned he had suffered a bad experience with me, sufficient to put him off having any such player in a significant role in the English game.

Part of what Albert suggested was right, his statement sat uncomfortably with me. I confess, as a Leeds United supporter and someone who held Don Revie in some esteem, I never thought of him having any negative bias towards his own Leeds United family. Sure, there were some issues with Gary Sprake after he sold 'alleged facts' about the Revie match fixing scandal to a national newspaper after he had been sold by the club and replaced by an altogether better goalkeeper in my opinion, in David Harvey. Yet by comparison, Albert had done nothing to deserve the sad reaction shown to him by his former boss at Leeds.

I saw the sadness in Albert's eyes when he recounted this encounter to me, it clearly upset him to be so dismissed by a man he once admired and respected.

It is true that Don Revie didn't once call up (for an international cap) a black player during his time as England manager, indeed, Albert appears to be the only black player he did sign in his time at club level, though it should be remembered that this was based on someone else's initial introduction and judgment.

I like to think of Don Revie as a rounded and reasonably well balanced manager, albeit a superstitious one, a man who always did his best for Leeds United and looked after his staff. Where the England national team is concerned, there are many national team managers who haven't used black players; that doesn't make them partisan or biased towards white footballers or anti-black footballers. To be fair to Don Revie, good black footballers were few and far between in England in the 1960s era. Albert, with his ball skills and pace, was unique and very much a one-off, so perhaps the Leeds boss can be forgiven for not signing players for the sake of it, no matter what colour the player's skin may be, if they weren't good enough and didn't meet the strict Leeds United criteria, then with little fuss, they were moved on. Albert's own brother, Trevor, was given a trial period at the club, unfortunately for him, he didn't reach the Revie standard or show the potential of his brother and was moved on.

It is worth mentioning that Revie did look to South Africa for football talent that would enhance his team. In 1967, 16-year-old Bernard Hartze had trials at Leeds. In South Africa, Hartze had been categorised as being part of the coloured group, and had shown supreme ball skills and football quality when representing Sundowns (now Mamelodi Sundowns). At Leeds Don Revie told the youngster, that to sign him he had to have won seven caps for South Africa, which he hadn't. Thereafter, he could offer an apprenticeship with no promise of a professional contract at the end of this spell. Hartze left the club and was to later argue that he had been dealt an unfair hand by Revie and Leeds United. 'I was not allowed to play for my country then because of the apartheid laws in the 1960s, so where was I supposed to get seven caps from?'

Hartze's interviewer, Aboobaker 'Boebie' Williams claimed, 'Revie and Leeds had the opportunity to make a statement against a crime against humanity and do it for football reasons.'

The other South African players to come over to Leeds for trials were Percy 'Chippa' Moloi and Rashid 'Dynamite' Khan. None of them made the grade, each of them claimed that racism was more rife and virulent in England than it then was in South Africa. Those same players realised how tough a life it was for Albert Johanneson, and with no support from within the football club or society he was left to deal with racist taunts and abuse himself.

I don't believe Don Revie was racist, he was a man focused on success, a man who recognised a good footballer from an average one. In the 1960s he was just one of an entire population who had no idea of the pressures placed upon a black man in a white society, let alone on the football field. Revie was a selfish man, he simply did what he felt was right for Leeds United and not for anyone else.

Another player to have trials at Leeds was the fantastically named 'Ginger Pencil' who was another black South African. Ginger played for the Broken Hill club and was so named because of his slight pencil-like frame and dyed ginger hair. A supporter once called him 'Ginger Pencil' and he liked it so much that he adopted it as his title. At Leeds, he failed to inspire and was sent back. Albert recalled Ginger with great fondness.

> He was a striking looking man, fit and agile, he could run faster than most athletes I knew. His problem was his gregarious nature, he just wouldn't and didn't know how to shut up and sometimes he repeated things he should never have mentioned. His eagerness to learn and develop was sometimes seen as immaturity by the management. It didn't happen for him and he was sent back, I felt sorry for him, but Ginger didn't care, he was a man who lived for the moment, not for the future. Mr Revie liked to see long term focus and commitment from his overseas trialists, and that was something Ginger certainly didn't have.
>
> Rashid 'Dynamite' Khan was another who felt that Revie lacked any understanding for the plight of the black footballer in England. Rashid was upset that despite being a stranger to the city, he had to make his own way to the ground for training games. He asked Don Revie why the club could not give them the cost of bus fare to help them get around. The boss told him that he wasn't interested in learning about his transport problems, he was a trialist

who had to be at the ground at a certain time, if he couldn't manage that, then he wasn't any good to him or Leeds United. Rashid left not long after the discussion.

There were some decent black footballers back in the 1960s. Likewise, many are in the game now. Laurie Cunningham for example, he was a great kid, I liked him a lot, his game reminded me so much of my own. He was fleet of foot and had great skill and talent. I think he will always be remembered as one of the best ever black footballers to grace the English game. I met Laurie a couple of times, and was thrilled when he told me that he based his game on my own and that I had been inspirational to his own career in the game. I never thought of it that way. He moved to Real Madrid in a big money transfer. When I was told that he had been killed in a car crash I couldn't believe it, such a tragic loss of a wonderful talent.

Cyrille Regis is another good player, a bit like Clyde Best used to be, ruthless, powerful and tough; you wouldn't want to clash with them. Clyde was a footballer who I thought would go on to make a big name for himself, but like me he suffered much racist abuse. He always made me smile because he was such a lumbering giant, he sometimes looked awkward with the ball, then, when you least expected it, he would thump a shot into the top corner of the goal and you would realise he had bags of skill. John Barnes is popular and skilful, but he's not a patch on Laurie Cunningham.

There was also John Charles at West Ham, a decent enough, if not average kind of defender. We weren't ever on good terms and over the years he has had a few goes at me for the way I have led my life. I used to call him a right 'Charlie' for having the audacity to tell me how to live my life. I tried to explain to him the difference between being a black footballer from overseas and black footballer from Canning Town, in London. Charlie knew the English culture, he grew up in it, if he had gone to live in the townships in South Africa he would have struggled to understand the way of life. Don't get me wrong, we are both black, and neither of us were wholly accepted as being equal to white people, not here, nor in South Africa. But Charlie didn't suffer the verbal and physical abuse I did, he got off lightly from what I have heard, but saying that, he got abuse too and there was no need for it at all.

There have been a couple of black goalkeepers too like Alex Williams who was at Manchester City. He is one who stood out, he was as athletic and strong as any goalkeeper I know; perhaps more so because being so close to the crowd for much of the time he must have heard and suffered much bad language and name calling. It's a curious thing but I don't think I have ever spoken to a black footballer in England who hasn't suffered some form of racist insult. It's a sad world we live in.

My hope would be for a world where everyone is seen as equals and where people from all cultures can live and work together in harmony. If football can sort itself out and portray a clean image, especially on the football pitch, then the right message can be communicated across the world. Am I asking too much for football to at least try, do you think?

Not long after this interview came the news that Albert had passed away in his tiny flat at number 16 Gledhow Towers, Leeds. Rumours abound that his body lay undiscovered for a number of days. In truth it matters little, the world had lost a football hero, a legend and a family had lost a loved one who can never be replaced. The cause of death was officially recorded as: bronchopneumonia, acute meningitis and cardiomyopathy.

Shortly after, I attended Albert's funeral at Lawns Wood cemetery, Leeds. It was a sombre affair, and I confess to shedding more than a few tears, I was not alone in doing so. The then chairman of Leeds United, Leslie Silver, a good man in his own right, kindly subsidised a headstone for Albert's final resting place. Each time I return to Leeds, I religiously call in to visit Albert, and to thank him for all he did for my football club and for football in general. In life he thrilled hundreds of thousands of people across the world with his dazzling football skills, in death he remains respected by generations of Leeds United supporters everywhere.

For me personally, he has my utmost respect for not only being a damn good footballer, but for being one of the bravest and strongest people I know. Meeting him so many times and getting to know him was one my greatest achievements. His recollections and anecdotes changed my way of thinking about diversity and perceptions of life in general. Let us never lose sight of the fact that Albert Johanneson was a great man who, through no fault of his own, lost his way. He is very much more than the media portrayal of him.

God bless you Albert.

# Statistics

Full Name:          Albert Louis Johanneson
Date of Birth:      13 March, 1940
Place of Birth:     Johannesburg, South Africa
Height:             1.70m (5ft 7ins)
Playing position:   Left Winger

**Career**:

**Leeds United**: 1961 – 1970: 172 appearances, 48 goals in all competitions
Debut appearance v Swansea Town (Elland Road) 8 April 1961
Last appearance v Burnley (Elland Road) 4 April 1970

**York City**: 1970 – 1972: 26 appearances, 3 goals in all competitions
Debut appearance v Notts County (Bootham Crescent) 15 August 1970
Last appearance v Bristol Rovers (Bootham Crescent) 14 August 1971